THE ENTREPRENEUR'S GUIDE SERIES

HOW TO TURN YOUR IDEA INTO A
MULTI-MILLION
DOLLAR BUSINESS

AND AVOID THE MISTAKES THAT SEND MOST NEW BUSINESS OWNERS INTO BANKRUPTCY!

JOHN MILLAR

I dedicate this book to my mother and father, who raised me while self-employed. They taught me to work hard and listen to everyone but to make my own choices as to what is right and what is wrong…and oh, did I mention to work hard? Anyone who tells you to work smart not hard hasn't ever done it tough and realized that if you work smart AND hard you will achieve more than you can possibly dream.

ISBN-13: 978-1497444331
ISBN-10: 1497444330

As a charity we have had hundreds of people over the years that have good intentions towards helping the young people that we deal with. Not everybody can walk the talk. One of the stand out things about John is that he not only talks about strategies and ways to help but he actually walks it out and delivers it every time.

I have no hesitation in recommending this book and the strategies contained here within, as I know they will help grow you and your business.

Not only is John adding value to you with this book, but he is also adding value to the next generation by donating all of the profits from the sale of this book in perpetuity, to our charity Bridge Builders.

We are blessed to know John, and he is helping us help hundreds of young people.

Regards,
Phil Stenhouse OAM
CEO
Bridge Builders Youth Organization

ALL profits from the sales of this book are being donated to
www.bridgebuilders.com.au

Contents

FOREWORD

I am honored to have been asked to write this foreword for John's book. I have only known John for a little over 4 years, and I find his personality infectious. His zest and passion for anything he tackles is so much needed in today's society, where it is so easy to be negative and be a doomsayer. I applaud his attempt at putting on paper his enthusiasm for helping people, from many walks of life.

You only need to read the many testimonials in the book to understand how affective John has been at communicating his message.

To me, after reading this book, John has captured the real essence of not only starting a new business, but the key areas of running a successful business. The book covers all aspects of owning your own business. The only thing it doesn't cover is how to spend your profit.

I have attended countless seminars over the years, where business guru's told me how easy it was going to be to make a buck. I have also read many publications on different aspects of running a business, but none have quite captured me like this book.

It is a carefully written, methodical, step-by-step approach to owning a business and what I really like is its "plain English" no nonsense vocabulary.

I have always said "you don't have to be a brain surgeon to be in business, but you have to have a will to succeed". I think this book encourages you to have a go, roll up your sleeves and do it. Because when the going gets tough and it will from time to time, roll the sleeves up a little higher.

John's passion for a positive outcome and his matter of fact solutions to problem solving are great lessons to take from this book.

My two sons, Robert and Cameron, are actively involved in my business and they will attest to the fact that a little hard work never killed anyone.

I don't quite know how John has found the time to be so active in his career, write a book, and have six children, but it does show he lives by his motto "whatever it takes".

This is a well written, easy to follow book on starting a business that follows the edict that you won't go broke making a profit. It is a good read for anyone who likes the idea of taking $1 and turning it into $2. John's a man of vision with an in-depth knowledge of the subject matter.

This book has been a fascinating read, even for someone like me who has been in his own business for over 40 years.

I recommend this book to you and remember to do "whatever it takes".

Bob Jones
Managing Director | Re-Car

INTRODUCTION

Starting Your Business

Since I first went into business over 26 years ago, I have seen far too many great people with great ideas go belly up and fail where other less competent and less talented individuals have survived. Some of this is simply due to pure dumb luck, and believe me I have seen some dummies get very lucky, but in the vast majority of cases, the reason a person succeeds or fails lies at the feet of the Rule of 6 P's:

"**P**rior **P**reparation **P**revents **P**itifully **P**oor **P**erformance!"

You could also say it this way: "An ounce of preparation will save you pounds of pain later."

This is top quality advice when applied to starting your own business, where you have so much to gain—and so much to lose. Think of starting a business as being comparable to building a home for your family. If you do not build the foundations correctly, the main structure will collapse and you could lose everything, not just your property, but other less evident things as well. I have seen people who suffered not only a business failure, but also the loss of their family, their fortune, their self-esteem, their dignity—and yes, in some instances, even their lives.

Here is an example of this that I will never forget. Several years back, I was referred to a business owner who was in some amount of trouble making ends meet. After spending just a short amount of time discussing my services, this potential client decided there was no need for a business coach at all, so we parted ways. A few months later, I happened to see a news report about this individual, who had been killed in a terrible car accident. The business was at that point insolvent. On the home front, things were also bad: the spouse had left the home, apparently distraught (according to the news report) after years of angst over the lack of money and the many hours they had spent on the failing business. This business owner ultimately turned to drugs and alcohol and wasn't accepting support from peers, many of whom had disavowed this person.

I know this story is sad, and I can't say for certain that the failed business led to such a terrible ending, but having first-hand knowledge of this person, and listening to the details of the news report did, in my mind, make it a high probability that the failed business venture was in large part to blame.

Optimism Abounds

It is often difficult for a new business owner to see all the potential pitfalls associated with a startup because they have so much enthusiasm for the venture and an unquench-able desire to be their own boss. In the eyes of the founder, business ownership has many benefits because success in business can lead to extreme wealth and (what appears to be) complete control over one's destiny. In reality, however, even the most successful business founders are never in complete control of their destiny because they still answer to someone or something. It may not be an overbearing boss standing at the doorway to an office full of cubicles demanding that you arrive every morning at 8 a.m. sharp; instead, it could a $10-million-dollar-a-year client needed by the business owner for the company to remain successful. As with most things in life, the "equation" of business ownership has both an upside and a downside as well.

Now that I have given you some of the doom and gloom, we can move on with the task at hand: showing you how to start a company properly. I will share with you some of what I share with a typical client who comes to me for coaching or consulting when they are planning to start a new business.

First of all, you must understand that it really doesn't matter how many companies a person has owned in the past (I have owned so many I have lost count). You must still follow the basic rules of business, and most of all it comes down to *planning*. As the old saying goes (and I'm sure you have heard it many times):

"If you fail to plan you plan to fail"

What should a person do to gain the knowledge needed to start a business?

Basically, you can take classes, read books, or get direction from a competent business coach or mentor. The biggest problem with getting this information from books is that so many books say a lot about nothing and nothing about a lot, or they are so busy force feeding their information that a reader doesn't know where to start. Add to that a countless number of coaches, who are essentially unskilled "vermin" and "predators" who spend all day promising the entire planet while delivering very little. These are the so called "business coaches" and "consultants" that have no real business sense or valid experience. In many instances, the only business they ever owned is their coaching or consulting business. Add to this the plethora of misinformation out there about what is actually required to start and run a successful business, and you start to see why (1) more businesses fail in the first two years of operation than survive, and (2) of those that do survive, the vast majority won't be around after five years.

I have written this book in simple English, making sure to present the basic steps in the order you must follow to start your business properly. The book offers a lot of information, but it also challenges you with many relevant questions. Take the time to think about and answer these questions carefully, and they will provide you with many of the answers you need to not only *survive* but to *thrive* in today's highly competitive marketplace.

I know your task is difficult. I coach business owners every day who are facing the same problems you will likely face when starting your business. The good news is that most of these problems can be overcome—or avoided entirely—if you start your business with a good foundation and proper planning. You can do so by soliciting advice EARLY ON from a competent business coach, accountant, and lawyer; then, as your business evolves, your team of helpers can evolve along with it.

Whether you are planning to start your 1st business or your 50th business let me be your guide. Walk with me on this exciting new journey. Grab a pen, notepad, and highlighters; then get ready to knuckle down and do it right the first time while we turn your idea into a multi-million dollar, highly profitable business together.

1   *MINDSET*

The Early Stages

I am sure you have heard the famous saying:

"The longest journey begins with a single step."

When I went into business for the first time, like many entrepreneurs, I jumped in boots and all at the opportunity to work for myself. Not only was I eager to run my own company and gain more control over my destiny, but I had also discovered that I did not fit in very well with my coworkers. I felt I was different than the typical employee: I wanted everything as quickly as possible; in fact "yesterday" was a good timeframe for me. Unfortunately, while this may be a positive attribute when it comes to being an entrepreneur and running your own company, it can create difficulties when you are tasked with working in a group as a member of a team. Had I worked for the right manager back then, it is possible that I might have been promoted to a leadership position, but lacking that, I often found myself in conflict with my coworkers. You could say I was a "self-starter," so I was a perfect candidate to launch a business of my own. This became quite a motivating factor to strike out on my own and do it "my way."

Other factors, beyond self-motivation, are critical to making it in the business world, including good coaching or mentoring. We all need mentors, in some form or another. I was *lucky* in many ways when I started out: I was *lucky* to meet some great business mentors; I was *lucky* after I ignored their advice and suggestions not to do anything that would prove fatal to my business; and I was *lucky* I learned how to get out of my own way early enough to really take things to the next level. More on this later.

I will soon list some of the important questions you should ask yourself before you launch a new business. These questions are formed around two very important questions for the business founder:

1) *Is being in business right for you?*
2) *Are you ready for business?*

Lots of businesses fail because the owner should never have been in business in the first place and/or because they were in the wrong *type* of business. By considering these questions, and going through the checklist at the back of this book, you can save yourself a tremendous amount of heartache later. I know this not only from first-hand knowledge, but from my experience helping clients transition their companies from the initial planning phases into operating a successful company in full stride.

Possibly you have seen on TV a show featuring a self-made millionaire. Watching this person, seeing the property they own and the life they lead, you may have wondered how someone can achieve so much from a world that seems so difficult. At first glance, this successful entrepreneur might appear to be a typical person since so many successful business owners do start out in average circumstances, meaning they are not rich, they have no large inheritance, or no ready-built company has been handed down to them from their forebears. This person, the focus of the TV show, probably started out just like you and I did, with not a whole lot given to us, but somehow they were able to "bootstrap" themselves into owning and operating their own company. Now they are very successful—as indicated by the lifestyle they lead and the property they own.

How did they get into such a position, one that seems so enviable?

This successful person gets to call all the shots, so they can set their own schedule, purchase almost any luxury item they desire, take a vacation to anywhere in the world. They appear to have it all, and life seems simple to them. What for most of us is an insurmountable problem (financial independence) has been solved by this person somehow.

But many of our assumptions here are not entirely true. While this individual may be able to purchase luxury items, they are most often "attached" to the company they have created, and they likely spend a very high percentage of their time tending after it. They cannot just hop on a plane and fly around the world on a whim, oblivious to the ebb and flow of the business they have founded. It is in fact likely that this person spends many hours to keep it all working, so many that they may not have taken a real vacation in years, unless you count working several hours a day from a laptop in the hotel room a real vacation. Unlike the typical "employee," who works at a company owned by someone else, this successful entrepreneur and business founder must keep his or her hand on the pulse of the business and be able to react to the sundry needs of a client on a moment's notice.

Don't get me wrong. I am not trying to talk you out of owning your own business, but I want you to be aware that with all of those wonderful things that seem so positive also come some things you might find somewhat negative.

Step 1: Is Business Right for You?

Before you take the first step toward starting your own business, carefully assess whether or not you are suitable to run your own business and if your head and heart are in the right place to be the leader of your own company. Let's not kid ourselves; you have to understand not just what you are planning to do, but *how* and most importantly *why* you are going into business.

The What

The "What" would be the *type of business* you are going into, and this is a huge factor because you should be well-equipped to go into that particular type of business. Running a pet store is a significantly different experience—requiring a different skillset—than running a night club. This is a two-way street. On one hand is you; on the other, the business. Think of starting and running your business this way: the experience will be comparable to entering into an intimate relationship, so you better be ready and willing to engage all the nuances that come with a particular business. For example, if you are starting that pet store, you should really like to be around animals.

You should also have the necessary skills to run the type of business you are starting. You can't run a technology company very well if you are computer illiterate and know nothing about technology, or worse if you are afraid of it. You might be able to manage a technology company, but it's not going to be easy, and certainly not fun, and this is usually a recipe for disaster.

The How

The "How" refers to all those steps involved in starting and running a particular type of company. Here, you not only need to have expertise in the section of business or industry you are entering, but you also need to have general business skills and acumen. This book is giving you those general skills, and these skills can apply to mostly any type of business. As I mentioned before, you will also need the assistance of various professionals, who can make up the difference between what you bring to the table and what is required in general business acumen.

I'm not going to say a lot here about those general requirements; instead, I have created this entire book and reading it will provide you with those skills and increase your chances significantly.

The Why

The "Why" is probably the most overlooked of these three single-word questions. Many people don't do the hard work necessary to think seriously about those reasons prompting them to found their new business; rather, they just rush off and start the new venture. *Voila!* And this often leads to a failure. Most entrepreneurs will attest to the fact that they had to start several companies—most of which failed partially or completely—BEFORE they were able to get it right. By the way, this book will help you avoid those failures, and that is my goal here: I want your very first business to succeed. Follow the advice herein and it will.

There is a famous saying that goes something like this: "Do what you love and the money will follow." I think most readers will agree that this seems generally true, so enough said. It is interesting and highly appropriate in this context, however, to consider the opposite of that statement (well, sort of the opposite):

"Do what you **HATE** and the money will **NOT** follow."

Meaning if you do not enjoy what you do for a living, you probably *will not* make much money doing it. This, however, is not entirely true because you may be in a job that pays very well, but you dislike the work so much that you are seeking to get out on your own and start your own business, for whatever reason. Suppose you are a highly paid computer programmer, but you always wanted to be an artist; that has been your dream and passion for years, but only a hobby until now. You earn a significant salary as a programmer, but you hate staring at code and fixing bugs, so you decide to follow your lifelong dream and start your own company with your artwork as the product of that business. The good news is that there are many things—as discussed herein—you can do to significantly improve your chances of succeeding as an artist, even if your artwork is not that good. The bad news is that if you are an extremely bad artist, and you do not possess the natural gifts you need to get better, all the business acumen in the world might not save you. It will however, notify you of all the steps you must take to succeed and give yourself the best chance possible. And if art (whatever flavor you are into) is your passion, you can still start a very successful company that deals with art—even though you may not be the artist creating the products of that business. Many other types of companies can give you some amount of satisfaction by allowing you to work *close to* the artwork you love. You could sell the artwork of others, for example. The key thing here is that you really need to think about the business you are starting and why you are doing it.

It is usually not good enough to say: "I am starting my artist company because I hate programming" and leave it at that. Maybe you hate programming, but what else is at stake? Possibly, being a programmer subjects you to so much stress that you feel it is detrimental to your health and you will soon die if you cannot lower the stress levels associated with meeting programming deadlines and saving the day by fixing the large-system crashes you are responsible to fix. The latter reason—saving your health—makes starting your own company a much more viable alternative to being a programmer than just "because I hate programming." Knowing these deeper, more important reasons will help you get your mindset right since you will better understand what is at stake in your new venture.

If you really think these things through—answering the questions posed in this section and in the Appendix will help you do so—you will gain a better understanding of your reasons for striking out on your own, and you need this insight to continue. Too many new business owners fail in this respect, and by the time they realize the real reasons, it is often too late to change the business model.

To gain insight into your motivations for starting a business, first answer the below questions in your mind; then take the time to write these answers down on a piece of paper. The act of writing will help clarify your thinking.

Will the Business Satisfy My Needs Financially?
» Why am I thinking of going into business?
» Have I discussed this with my family?
» What are my current financial needs?
» How much do I need the business to provide and by when do I need the business to provide this?

Do I Have the Necessary Skills and Experience?
» What experience do I have?
» What training and education have I completed?
» What experience is necessary for this particular type of business?
» What will be the most difficult thing to do in this type of business?

Do I Have a Sound Business Proposition?
» Have I prepared a formal business plan?

- » What obstacles and challenges do I anticipate?
- » Have I identified a target market?
- » What will make my business stand out from the competition?
- » Can I acquire the licenses and permits needed to run my business?
- » Will I have the finances and resources to start and run my business for an adequate amount of time?
- » What is an adequate amount of time before the business will be self-sustaining?
- » Where will the funding come from?
- » How much will it cost to start my business?
- » What are all the expenses I will need to meet?
- » Which expenses will be most critical to keeping the business running?
- » What parameters will I use to measure my success?
- » What business reports will tell me if I am doing well or not?
- » What steps do I need to take next?
- » Do I have my support team in place: (1) a competent business coach, (2) an accountant, (3) a bookkeeper, (4) a financial planner and (5) a business banker?

Take the time to write down your answers to these questions. I know this works because I didn't consider any of these questions when I first went into business. I just saw the opportunity and jumped in, which is what most people do when they get carried away in the excitement of starting a new company. The result for me was that my business was in chaos. I had good sales in my products but no idea whether or not I was actually making any profit. I was working around the clock, seven days a week, churning away like crazy and hoping things would turn out. I thought for sure with all the products and services I was delivering that I had to be doing well. In reality, however, I had no idea what was and wasn't working and I felt like I was just working to keep all the balls in the air—like a circus juggler.

Had I taken the time to think about and answer the above questions, I would have been better equipped to measure my success and make critical decisions about how I needed to run the business.

Had I taken the time *before I started the business* to think about the parameters I would need to measure the performance of the business, and had I developed some relevant reports to measure that performance, I would have known exactly how I was doing. Since I did not, I was essentially operating in the blind. I might as well have been speeding down a busy freeway in a big truck wearing a blindfold, pedal to the metal. In that instance, I got lucky my business did not end in a tremendous crash, as I have seen so many other new startups do. In that startup I was extremely lucky: despite my incompetence, my lack of knowledge, and the improper systems and planning, I didn't go broke. I did go on to realize my mistake (and how lucky I was), so this near-miss taught me to do the opposite for my next business venture, which grew faster, was more profitable, and had better cash flow. Best of all, I worked half the hours!

Step 2: Are You Ready for Business?

Is it now or not right now?

Many businesses fail due to a lack of planning and preparation. But there is another key factor: timing. Before starting a business, make sure you are ready. All of us want immediate satisfaction. We want what we want *right now* and with no delays! This is how life is getting, and this phenomenon is due to several factors, like the progression of technology and the increased connectivity of society. We no longer take the time to think and plan our communications; rather, we just tap in a text message and push SEND. Ooops! It is not so easy to take these messages back; in fact, there is no way to UNSEND. This might be forgivable in our personal communications, but in business it can be fatal. So avoid the impulse to just launch into your business; take the time to consider if this is the right time to start your company. You need to know whether it is time to go all out and start your business or if it's better to delay your plans for a while in case you are not quite ready yet.

As with the above questions, answer the below questions in your mind and then take the time to write these answers down on a piece of paper. The act of writing will help clarify your thinking.

Starting Your Business
  - » Which business structure will I use?
  - » Have I identified what roles need to be filled within my company?
  - » Have I thought of registering a business name?
  - » Do I understand my tax obligations?
  - » What marketing strategies will I use and why?
  - » What insurance will I need and how much will it cost?
  - » Are there any other legal issues related to my business?
  - » Where will my offices be located and who will be my suppliers?

Operating Your Business
  - » Have I thought about cash flow and record keeping?
  - » How will I manage the performance of my employees?
  - » How will I manage debt in my business?
  - » Do I understand my obligations towards my employees?

» Have I developed an exit and succession plan?

Business Assistance

» Do I know where to find help, advice, and assistance?
» Are there any grants or other financial assistance programs available to my business?
» Have I identified my five pillars? These are my accountant, my bookkeeper, my business coach, my finance broker or business banker, and last but not least my financial planner.

On a final note, the reality is that most businesses won't make you wealthy, but if you run them properly they will spin the cash flow wheel and generate profits that allow you to invest in those things that will make you truly wealthy. Knowing the *Whats*, the *Hows*, and *Whys* of your particular business venture is more important than ever, and to do so you must ask yourself the questions posed in this chapter.

2 | *CASH FLOW IS KING!*

You have probably heard the saying:

"Knowledge is power"

In business, this is very true, and this power often comes in unexpected ways. I have to admit that I really didn't like math when I was in school, and I used to rag on all the kids who did. I couldn't see the sense in it until I started my first business and realized that the better I knew my numbers, the more money I could make. Although I am still not a big fan of math per se, at least now I can see why knowledge—in this case, the ability to do math—can be so powerful.

In this chapter, you will learn about various financial topics, including cash flow (the most important), securing finance, key accounting information, budgeting, and taxation.

Step 3: Securing Financing

To secure financing for your business, you need to assess your financial requirements and identify available funding sources, including any potential government grants and assistance programs. You also need to understand the typical requirements and the information you need to prepare when applying for financing.

The famous rock band, The Beatles, once said: "Money can't buy you love," but baby let me tell you, if you don't have enough startup money to buy the assets you need and to fund your cash flow (at least in the beginning phases of your startup), you just might be finished before you really get started. This is a common rookie mistake I see new business owners making. They lose sight of financial considerations, ending up with lots of profitable sales they are unable to fund—ironically, leading to a failure.

Assessing Your Financing Requirements

When starting a business, one of the first and most critical points to address is to identify all the potential costs you will face. These costs generally fall into two categories:

1) *Start-up costs* - the initial outlays when setting up your business, such as shop upgrades, equipment purchases, licensing outlays.
2) *Ongoing costs* - the recurring costs necessary to run and maintain the business, such as wages and rent.

It is also very important to consider including an allowance of cash, or "float," as working capital for the early stages when you may not necessarily be generating enough revenue to cover all your costs. Maintaining some spare funds will help you cover any unexpected expense fluctuations until you can build up a sufficient cash reserve.

Sources for Financing

Various financing sources exist, each with their own benefits and costs. Carefully evaluate your specific requirements and determine which financial options are best suited to your needs. I will present you with some financial funding alternatives in this section. Get your finances in order early on and you can really fly.

There are two critical factors related to financing: first, debt isn't a bad thing if it is *serviceable* debt (meaning you can afford the periodic payments), and second it's better to have financing available and not need it than need it and not have it! Make sure you are in a position of strength so you don't have to go, cap in hand, begging for pennies when things get tight. As with insurance, it's better to have it in place and never need it than need it and not have it.

Some of the typical financing options for business ventures include:

» *Personal Savings* – Many people choose to use their retirement funds to help with the costs of launching a new business. This is risky, but if your idea is solid, you may want to do it. I am sure you have heard the countless stories about those individuals who used all their savings, opened a business, and ultimately became very successful. It sounds good when someone else is doing it, but when you put your retirement on the line, make sure you do all your research first. If possibly, you can borrow from your retirement account rather than taking a loan at the bank or withdrawing the money outright. Some account managers will manage this "self-loan" by issuing the loan and managing the payment you make back into the retirement account. This can get you a good interest rate and all the proceeds ultimately go back to you.

» *Credit Cards* – Credit cards do provide a quick, easy source of funds to run the business. The problem with using credit cards to fund a business is that credit card debt can easily—and very quickly—become unserviceable debt, or an out of control obligation you are unable to repay. The interest rates are steep and various triggers exist such that if you miss a single payment by even a day, the rates can skyrocket, not just for the card you missed the payment on, but on *all your credit cards*. You might as well be resting your head in a "financing guillotine." Unlike not being able to repay a loan from your retirement account, missing payments on a credit card will also adversely affect your credit rating—and thus your ability to obtain credit in the future.

» *Friends and Relatives* – This is another common source for new business funding. The problem with tapping into friends and family is that you may strain the relations with loved ones if you are unable to repay the debt. In a sense, you are borrowing against those relationships and they are part of the collateral for the loan. Those family outings might get even more stressful than they are now and the relations a bit more strained if unpaid loan money comes into play.

» *Angel Investors* – The issue here is that you will add a sort of "glass house" atmosphere to your company such that others will become involved in your operations. What I mean by glass house is that you will need to operate more transparently so the investors can see everything as it unfolds. This can increase the stress because those outside forces can make demands or try to impose changes in your operations. Maybe you do not want that added stress during the initial phases of your startup. This can also be a good thing because the increased visibility keeps you more accountable. Those outsiders looking in may see some of the problems before you do and they may be able to give you advice to help correct the situation. You do, however, lose a certain amount of freedom since you need to appease these investors, who in many cases don't know hardly as much as you do about the particular type of business you are starting.

» *Leases* – The tradeoff with leasing is that you will be putting a lot of cash into the *expense* side of the business rather than the *asset* side. Think of it this way: would you rather (1) rent an apartment to live in or (2) buy a house using credit? If you buy it, your house will (in all likelihood) gain in value and someday you will not need to make any house payments and you can use the rent money for something else. The subtlety here is that even when you take out a loan to buy a property, the bank in essence still owns it until you make the last payment. This option does give you more control than a lease however, because your name is also on the title, and unlike a rental or lease property, there is no manager breathing down your neck or threatening to exercise the exit clause in the lease. With option 2, if property valuations trends continue up as they have historically, your net worth will rise with the value of the property, and so your business will have increased in value. This is something you can monetize when/if you sell. You will be more attached to the property with option 2; on the other hand, if you rent, you can move easily and you are not stuck if property values fall. Lease payments are also typically a bit higher than mortgage payments.

» *Bank Loans* – Here, as with using funds from investors, you need to answer to someone for the money you have borrowed. Banks will be less intrusive than investors in the day-to-day operations, but if you default they will also foreclose on whatever assets you put up to secure the loan. If you used your personal home as collateral, and your business fails, you will risk losing it. Compare this to borrowing money from your rich granddad. He will likely not boot you out onto the street if you go belly up, but Christmas dinner may be a little sketchy at the end of the year!

Other Funding Sources
Grants and Assistance

Grants and other funding programs may be available from the federal, state and territorial governments and in some cases from local councils. Generally there are no grants available for starting a business; however, there are grants and other assistance programs for activities such as expanding your business, training, research and development, innovation and exporting.

This seems amazing to me considering how much effort you must put into getting a driver's license so you don't crash and burn while driving your shiny new car. In comparison, it's almost ridiculous how easy and cheap it is to start a company that has the ability to crash and burn your life.

Assessing Your Financing Options

To ensure that you are getting the best deal on the best possible products, it is a good idea to research the different types of loans offered to small businesses by banks and other lenders. With a finance broker, you can compare interest rates, fees, and terms as well as any other associated costs to find the best deal for your business needs across a variety of lenders. Do not get locked into the products a particular bank or financial institution may have at the time you start your business.

It's also a good idea to watch for special offers, because it may make sense to take advantage of them, and don't be afraid to negotiate—the market for financing is very competitive, so it's worthwhile pushing hard to minimize your lending costs.

Applying for a Loan

If you decide to apply for a loan, be sure that you accurately prepare all the necessary documents and information the bank or financial institution needs to process your application. Loan applications require many details, including:

» A description of your business
» Your personal credit history
» The amount and purpose of the loan
» A repayment schedule
» Financial statements, or projected financial statements for a startup
» Security or personal guarantee

Lack of cash flow and under-capitalization (not enough starting and working capital) are the two biggest killers of businesses young and old, so don't gloss over this section. many people have come before you knowing full well the importance of cash flow; even so, what killed their business during startup?

Cash flow problems.

Hopefully by now your checklists and plans are getting bigger and better. Let us take a wander through the "land of nod" where accountants can speak gobbledy gook and give you some really simple but powerful concepts that, if you better understand them, will allow you to ask your accountant and bookkeeper more informed questions. These professionals really can be your best friends in business, and talking in their lingo will help you build a longer-lasting and more meaningful relationship.

Step 4: Understanding Key Accounting Information

To successfully operate your small business, you need to understand the following key accounting concepts before you take a single step further, so grit your teeth and hold on tight. This may be difficult, but I promise it will be worth it.

Assets

Assets are those items owned by your business that have a commercial value and are used to generate revenue, such as cash, inventory, production machinery, office equipment, vehicles, and buildings.

Liabilities

Liabilities are financial obligations that your company has to its creditors, such as loans and purchases made on credit.

Equity

Equity is the amount left over after you have deducted total liabilities from total assets. It is classified into two categories; capital contributions and retained earnings. Don't worry too much about understanding all the nuances here for the time being; just think of it as your net worth, or how much the business is worth.

Balance Sheet

A balance sheet is made up of three sections: (1) assets, (2) liabilities, and (3) equity. It summarizes your company's financial position at a point in time by providing a snapshot of what you own, what you owe to your creditors, and the difference between those two.

Income

Income represents the total amount of money that your business makes within a period of time. You can work out your business income by calculating your revenue, gains, and losses.

Cost of Goods Sold (COGS)

The cost of goods sold (COGS) are those costs directly

attributed to the production of a product. This includes the total cost of purchasing materials and paying for the labor required to manufacture the product. Any indirect or downstream costs, such as marketing or distribution, are not included in COGS.

Expenses

Expenses are all of the financial outlays a business makes during a time period, such as the utility bills, wages, and distribution expenses.

Profit and Loss Statement

A profit and loss statement is a summary of the income and expenses of a business. It shows the profit made during a given period of time (usually annually, quarterly, or monthly). A profit and loss statement can be used to identify areas of high expenditure that are unproductive in generating profit, or potential cash flow threats.

Breakeven Analysis

Your business breaks even if it generates enough sales income to cover its operating expenses. Any amount above the breakeven point is a *profit*. If a business makes less than the breakeven point, it incurs a loss. The point at which your revenues exceed your expenses is when you start making money (you exceed "breakeven"); until then, it is costing you money to be in business.

I always encourage my clients to know what day of the month they break even so we can strategize on ways to reduce the time required to reach breakeven, even if it is by one day at a time. In some businesses, it may be appropriate to work out the exact time of day on the day you break even. This helps to give the business owner a deeper understanding of the revenues and expenses, and what drives them.

OK, we made it through the accounting, and I hope you

are still with me and your eyes have stopped bleeding. You should have a better understanding about these critical financial concepts, and you will be pleasantly surprised later to discover how much you will use and rely on these.

Step 5: Cash Flow is "KING"

Why do I say "Cash Flow Is KING"?

The answer is simple: Cash flow is the single biggest cause of business failure in existence. Far too many very profitable businesses have gone under because they were asset rich but cash poor, meaning they had a *negative cash gap* or a cash flow cycle that was rampant and out of control. When this happens, you will often hear people say things like this:

"Sales are through the roof, and my accountant tells me I am profitable, but I don't have any money in the bank…"

Let me explain. Cash flow is the measure of money flowing into and out of your business at any given time. In an ideal business cycle, you will always have more cash flowing in than flowing out. The reality, however, is that most businesses must produce or deliver goods/services to their customers while paying their staff and suppliers BEFORE they get paid themselves. This lag in payments in and payments out is often a major challenge for the business, and managing it correctly is critical to the immediate financial health and long-term financial sustainability of the business. This amount—cash coming in and cash going out—is commonly known as a "cash gap."

The task of managing cash flow increases in complexity as the number of transactions and volume of money involved grows. This complexity can adversely affect the business if not managed properly.

Here is a simple test to measure the "health" of the cash flow in a business. A company should always have enough cash available to pay all wages and bills on time. When businesses cannot do this, they can face a "cash crisis" and the overall cash flow health is not so good. A cash crisis can make it difficult for the business to access supplies and will potentially disrupt their operations and ability to generate revenue. This in turn can kill a business very quickly.

Cash Inflows and Outflows

To understand the concept of cash flow more deeply, let's take a closer look at cash inflows and cash outflows. Cash *inflows* are any receipts of cash into a business. They can include:

» Customer payments for goods or services
» Receipt of a bank loan
» Interest on savings and investments
» Shareholder investments
» Tax refunds
» Proceeds from the sale of assets

Cash *outflows* are any cash outgoings and can include:

» Purchase of stock, raw materials, or equipment
» Wages, rents, and daily operating expenses
» Loan repayments
» Income tax, payroll tax, and other taxes
» Asset purchases

Clear as mud? You really need to understand these cash flow concepts if you want your business to survive and thrive (obviously you do!). For further understanding, and access to some valuable tools to assist you, check out the online training we have developed at *www.moreprofitlesstime.net*.

Step 6: Budgeting

A budget allows you to plan, control, and make decisions related to the assets, resources, and financial commitments of the business. Without a budget, your business may run the risk of spending more money than it is generating in revenue, or not spending enough to allow your small business to grow.

Budgeting allows you to:
- » Manage your finances effectively
- » Monitor the performance of your business
- » Obtain funding for your business
- » Benchmark your financial goals
- » See potential problems earlier so you can take corrective actions

There are many different types of budgets you can prepare (or have a competent professional prepare) for your business. It is critical that you prepare a budget that best reflects the needs of your business. The following represent the main types of budgets:
- » Projected Profit and Loss Statement
- » Projected Balance Sheet
- » Cash Flow Budget
- » Marketing Budget

When preparing a budget, be sure to consider the following issues:
- » As a budget is used as a guide for the finances of your business, it is important to ensure that it is prepared properly. Set aside ample time to prepare your budget; then update it regularly, or whenever necessary.
- » Be realistic in your budgets. Use historical figures (if available) as a guide to help you budget costs and sales. However, always remember that historical data is only a *guide*, so you must try to anticipate any factors and changes that can influence the future and make it different than the past.

» Allow for unforeseen expenditures. It is inevitable that your business may at some point be faced with expenses that were not originally planned for. It is a good idea to allow for some funds to be allocated as a contingency to meet unexpected costs.

» Include input from other staff members when preparing the budget. They may be able to assist in determining more realistic figures. Further, when staff members are included in this process, they are more likely to be motivated to help achieve targets.

For more information on the budgeting process, and tools to assist you, visit *www.moreprofitlesstime.net*.

Step 7: Taxation

I have yet to meet anyone who likes the tax man; not even other tax men like tax men, but when starting a business, you will be obliged to register your business for tax purposes. You will need to check with the appropriate tax authority in your country or region. As an example, here are some things that you may need in order to register your business in Australia:

» Australian business number (ABN)
» Fringe benefits tax (FBT)
» Goods and services tax (GST)
» Tax file number (TFN)

The USA counterpart to this list would be:

» Federal Employee ID Number (EIN)
» State Registration of your business entity
» Assumed Business Name (ABN) registered with the state

Depending on your location, you may also need to understand your obligations with respect to:

» Capital Gains Tax (CGT)

» Excise duties
» Fringe Benefits Tax (FBT)
» Goods and Services Tax (GST)
» Income tax for business
» International Tax
» Land tax
» Pay As You Go (PAYG) withholding
» Payroll tax
» Rates
» Stamp duty
» Superannuation for employees

This will vary based upon the country or countries you plan to operate in, but most countries have similar entities/ obligations. Always check with a competent accountant or financial planner (many are accountants also) in the venue you will operate in. Apart from these, there are a number of possible tax concessions and rebates that may be available for your business if:

» You are an individual, partnership, company, or trust;
» You are carrying on a business; and
» You have an aggregated turnover of less than $2 million.

The benefits of these concessions include:

» A choice to account for GST on a cash basis
» Simplified trading stock rules
» Simpler depreciation rules
» Immediate deductions for certain prepaid business expenses
» Entrepreneur's Tax Offset (ETO)

This is where your accountant and bookkeeper should shine to keep you compliant and on the happy side of the tax man. Personally I speak to my bookkeeper weekly, and at least monthly to my accountant. This way I can make sure I keep abreast of my businesses and things don't go too far astray before I can take corrective action to get things back on track if they have wandered.

Don't limit using your accountant and bookkeeper for compliance issues only; they are usually involved with many other companies, so they can be knowledgeable business advisors. They can help you plan. In fact, you, your business coach, your accountant, your finance broker, your bookkeeper, and your financial planner should be the very best of friends and meet together as a team regularly so you get the most from their advice and services.

3 LEGAL & COMPLIANCE

Now we step things up a notch to a discussion of your business lawyer. Since there are so many facets of the law and of the entire legal field it is too complex to master entirely. Lawyers are generally only experts in those legal areas they specialize in, so make sure you get someone who specializes in business law (rather than divorce, for example). You wouldn't ask a plumber to look at your light switch just because they are a tradesman would you? Lawyers are no different and don't make that mistake. If you will be operating your business in different countries, by all means establish a relationship with an attorney in each location.

Another thing to remember is you don't need a disaster before you contact a lawyer. My original understanding when I started my first business was that lawyers should only be consulted when things go wrong. This is far from the truth. Quite often, they can answer your questions and put things in place *before* anything bad happens, so they allow you to be proactive and prepare for potential trouble. As mentioned throughout this book, being successful in business requires planning, and this is true in the legal department as well. Work with your attorney *now* so you avoid having dramas *later*. Lawyers aren't just there to pop a band aid on your legal knee when you have a tumble!

There are many important legal and compliance issues that you really need to consider and make decisions on, so discuss these with your lawyer and understand them before you start your business. In this chapter, we provide an overview of the high-profile issues. They are business structures, registration, important legislation, and risk management.

Step 8: Business Structures

Prior to starting your business, you must decide on the business structure that best suits your needs. Factors to consider as part of this process include:

» The type of business you will be operating
» Establishment fees and maintenance costs
» Tax obligations
» The level of asset protection you require

To make this process even more complicated, you have several business structures to choose from when you plan your business. Each of these business types has a set of pros and cons. I will present the general structures below. Note that in different countries, these structures differ slightly, but in general we are talking about the same type of thing. Most of the differences lie in who is responsible for business liabilities and how many individuals are in control. Your attorney and accountant will help you sort these out.

The different business types are:

» *Sole Trader (Australia) or Sole Proprietorship (USA)* - a type of business entity which is owned and run by a single individual who is fully responsible for all liabilities and commitments of the business. Here, "fully responsible" means the individual is personally liable for the transactions of the company. If the business owes money to a creditor, and fails to make good on the obligation, the creditor can go after the individual personally. This differs from some of the other structures in that they provide varying levels of "protection" for the business owner(s) personally.

» *Partnership* - a type of business entity in which partners (owners) share with each other the profits or losses of the business. Here again, as with the Sole Trader structure, the partners have limited protections built into the business structure. If they do not carry adequate insurance at the business level, they could end up being personally liable for various failures in the business.

» *Proprietary Limited Company (Australia), Limited Liability Company (USA), or a Corporation (USA)* - an independent legal entity able to do business in its own right. The shareholders own the company and directors run the company. The directors of a company, as well as company employees, can be shareholders.

» *Trust* - a business structure whereby the trustee holds property and earns and distributes income on behalf of the beneficiaries.

You may also decide to operate your business as a:

» *Franchise* - an agreement under which a franchisor licenses a franchisee to operate a developed method of doing business that is identifiably associated with the franchisor. The franchisor also provides ongoing guidance, systems, and assistance in return for periodic payment of fees and/or purchases. In a sense, when you decide to start your business as a franchise, you gain a fair amount of established branding/business knowledge in return for a franchise fee. The business will start with name recognition and you will not have to establish it. You may also have ready-made distribution channels. This can significantly decrease the amount of time you allocate to become profitable. You will, however, be in a tight relationship with the franchisee and your fortunes will go the way of theirs to some degree.

» *Independent Contractor* - an individual or entity that provides goods or services to another entity under terms specified in a contract. If you provide services to your clients, you might start out as an independent contractor until you build up a client list large enough to launch a more formal company using one of the larger business structures.

» *Home-Based Business* - a small business that operates from the business owner's home office. These types of companies are becoming more popular since the progression of technology—primarily the Internet, with its ability to facilitate communication—is making this more attractive as time passes. As computers become faster and more reliable, you are able to do more with your business via remote connections. The existence and evolution of "the cloud"—shared storage and processing resources—is a testament to this.

Keep in mind that your legal and tax obligations (and exposures) will vary depending on the type of business you choose to operate and the country in which you operate it, so obtain good quality advice *before* you start. Fail to do so, and you might get yourself into a predicament that could end your business. For example, many individuals want to include some level of personal protection in their business structure. If you have employees, and one of them gets into a car accident while making a delivery, you certainly do not want to be sued and have all of your personal retirement money taken by lawyers in a long, drawn-out court battle. To avoid such scenarios, you should form your company as a Limited Liability Company, or use one of the other business structures that afford protection of your personal assets. A big insurance policy may not be enough; savvy attorneys pride themselves on their ability to get into your personal assets.

In general, there is a little bit more overhead associated with setting up and running a business under a structure that provides you this inherent, built-in protection. You pay a little more in time and money, but you get to sleep better at night knowing that your personal assets are separate from those of the business.

It is very important that you carefully consider each business structure to determine which is best suited to your needs. If you fail in this respect, you can literally lose everything. Meet with your accountant, business advisor, business coach, financial planner, and possibly even a business lawyer to get it right the FIRST time. Did I mention get it right the FIRST time?

Step 9: Business Registration, Licenses & Permits

When you're starting up a new business you must find out what registration and license requirements apply to you in your region or country. This can be confusing and somewhat complex since local, state, territorial, and federal governments all handle the different registration and licensing needs for various aspects of your business. Not only is it complex now, but government over time tends to increase in complexity rather than simplify, so don't be surprised if you need the help of a professional. You can do some local research so that you understand your obligations in regards to:

» Registering your business name (if you want to be a sole trader, a partnership or a trust)
» Registering your business structure (if you decide to operate as a company)
» Registering your domain (if you want to trade online)
» Registering your trademark (if you want to legally protect your brand and stop others from trading with it)

Note that you may have to register in each individual region you are operating in, depending on local requirements. Please also be aware that registration of a business name, company name, or domain name does not in itself give you any proprietary rights—only a trademark can give you that kind of protection. To guarantee your ownership and right to use a mark, and ensure that you have exclusive rights to use your name now and in the future, throughout the world, register your business name as a trademark. If you are unsure of what or how to register, you should seek the professional advice of an accountant or solicitor. In fact, so much is at stake, I recommend that you do seek professional assistance with the registration of your marks. The process is somewhat convoluted so you don't want to take on the task yourself only to make a simple mistake that can cost you dearly in the future.

Every country differs, but in Australia as an example you may also need to register your business for:

» Australian business number (ABN)
» Fringe benefits tax (FBT)
» Goods and services tax (GST)
» Pay As You Go (PAYG) withholding
» Tax file number (TFN)
» Payroll tax

Head starting to hurt yet? If you are reading this book to prepare for your first business, I am guessing it's a challenge, but one worthy of your focus and attention for just a little longer.

Step 10: Important Legislation

Every country is different but as an example, in Australia, federal and state laws protect you, your business, and your customers from unfair trading practices and mishandling of personal information. These laws, together with industry codes of practice, help to ensure that your business operates fairly and competitively and that all consumers are adequately informed and protected.

You need to be aware of your rights and responsibilities in relation to the following:

» *Competition and Consumer Act, 2010 (CCA)* – CCA is the main legislation that ensures fair trading in the marketplace. It deals with almost every aspect of your business, including advertising, price setting, and transactions with other businesses or consumers. CCA also covers unfair market practices, industry codes of practice, mergers and acquisitions of companies, product safety, collective bargaining, product labeling, price monitoring, and the regulation of industries such as telecommunications, gas, electricity and airports.

» *State and Territory Fair Trading Laws* – Each state and territory also has its own fair trading laws, usually referred to as the Fair Trading Act, with consumer protection provisions much the same as those in the CCA. State and territory fair trading offices can give general advice on your business rights and obligations under fair trading laws. However, if you're unsure how fair trading laws apply to your particular situation, then I encourage you to obtain independent legal advice.

» *Privacy Act (In Australia)* – The Federal Privacy Act 1988 sets rules for businesses handling personal information. It also allows individuals to file a complaint if personal information is mishandled. The Privacy Act only applies to certain businesses, so if you are unsure about your rights and obligations, you should seek independent, professional legal advice.

Your business may also be required to comply with other legislation and regulations administered by (in Australia):

» Australian Competition and Consumer Commission
» Australian Taxation Office
» Australian Securities and Investments Commission

Each country will have its own variation of these government entities. Your accountant and/or attorney can assist you with this.

Step 11: Risk Management & Insurance

Risks can be good but only if you understand them and can control them; otherwise, they can be a detriment to your business efforts. When we take risks we do not fully understand, or that we do not have some level of control over, we increase the likelihood of a bad result occurring at some point. In a similar fashion, you would not go out and drive a car you did not know how to operate—or drive it in a reckless fashion—or you would eventually crash.

Risks to your business however can arise for many reasons, including interest rate or price increases, your competitors' activities, injuries resulting from hazards in the workplace, skilled staff leaving, natural disasters or terrorist activities. Some risks can be controlled and others cannot, but you better be prepared, or at least aware of them, before they sneak up and bite you on the proverbial behind.

Risk Management

Managing risk is an important part of running your business, and whether you tend to be bullish like me (i.e., able to tolerate more than the average amount of risk) or more conservative (i.e., favoring less risk), you will fare better in business if you take on the amount of risk that suits your appetite. This way you will not end up with what I refer to as "Risk Indigestion," which leads to worry and you becoming a generally cranky person.

Risk management is a process, in which you (1) determine the true level of risk to your business and (2) develop and implement strategies that allow you to manage and minimize the risk. Before you can properly manage your risks, they need to be identified. Begin with these questions:

» What can go wrong?
» What impact will it have on my business?
» What can we do to prevent it?
» What do we do if it happens?

Taking out an appropriate form of insurance—and the right dollar amount—is usually an effective risk management strategy for a small business. Having the proper type of insurance will protect your company from financial loss and minimize exposure to risk. You should research the different types of insurance available to your business, including:

» Asset and revenue insurance
» People insurance
» Liability insurance

Before signing up to any type of insurance policy, evaluate

its suitability and value in terms of your individual circumstances. Take the time to consider the following questions:

- » What is covered?
- » What is not covered?
- » Are you under-insured?
- » Do you understand the term "co-insurance"?
- » When does your protection commence?
- » What are the conditions of the insurance policy?
- » What are the claims procedures?
- » Do you understand the terms of a replacement policy?
- » What are the renewal conditions?
- » What is the reputation of the insurance company?
- » What differences do you find when you compare policies?
- » Are you prepared to negotiate pricing?

HUMAN RESOURCES & EMPLOYEE MANAGEMENT

4

If you intend to employ people in your small business, you'll need procedures for how you will hire, manage, and fire them effectively. You must do this *before* you hire them and not after, or you can encounter several problems, including not having the management skills, hiring the wrong person, or hiring the right people but putting them in the wrong job.

Don't just consider their skills; also look at their ability to grow, their value to your business, their commitment to your culture and goals, and their desire to go the extra mile for your business.

Your skills in recognizing and recruiting the best employees will develop over time, and there are plenty of resources and tools around to help you really nail this part of your business early on. To assist you, we have a series of online tools to help you test, evaluate, and benchmark new recruits and existing team members alike. Visit *www.moreprofitlesstime.com* to find a series of tools that take into account various aptitudes, including certain industry skills and knowledge, IQ, Emotional Intelligence, Sales Skills, management skills and more. In this

chapter, we present information about the basic considerations involved with employing people, your obligations,
employee entitlements, the recruitment process, and the
important legal issues.

Step 12: Hiring Considerations

The people working within your business each fall under
a category of employment. Each category has different
obligations for both you and your employees. The first step is
to determine whether your workers are classed as employees
or contractors.

An *employee* is someone who works under a contract of
employment.

Those who are not employees are referred to as *independent
contractors* or *sub-contractors*.

There are significant differences legally between the two
regarding awards, retirement, insurance and compensation.
In our coaching and training programs, we offer a number of
tools and training styles we use to help our clients determine
what type of workers they employ, when they employ them,
and what role they should be in.

It is important to establish the most suitable type of
employment for each individual situation when recruiting
new staff. The types of employment you may wish to consider
include:

» Full-time employees
» Part-time employees
» Casual employees
» Probationary employees
» Fixed-contract employees
» Contractors

You will note there is no category for slaves or bondsmen;

you should have an obligation to your team to consider them as your greatest asset.

There are many costs associated with employing people. It is important for you to take all of these costs into account during the employment process. Some of the costs that you will need to take into consideration include:

» Recruitment costs
» Training and development costs
» Wages
» Superannuation
» Annual leaves
» Sick leaves
» Maternity leaves
» Public holidays

Many small business owners make one or both of the following rookie mistakes: (1) hiring someone prematurely or (2) trying to save money by not hiring anyone (and attempting to do everything themselves). Both strategies are fraught with danger. If you are in doubt about how to proceed, it is best to err on the side of caution: don't hire someone. A miss-hire is one of the most expensive mistakes you will make during your early years. Instead, consider outsourcing; use contractors to do the job, preferably those who have some serious skin in the game, meaning they must perform or you can release them.

On top of these costs, in many countries you may be obliged to pay for insurance to cover Workers Compensation. Check to see if there is a variation of this in your country. Insurance expenses can vary greatly depending on the level of risk in your particular industry.

Employing new people also comes with a number of taxation requirements. These can vary from state to state and country to country, so you should visit the local tax authority and consult with your accountant for specific advice.

Step 13: Employer Responsibilities

In most countries, you have various obligations as an employer, including legal, paperwork and records, staff health and safety in the workplace, superannuation and taxation, anti-discrimination practices, dispute resolution, and insurance.

Legal. Your legal obligations relate to paying the correct wages to staff, reimbursing employees for work-related expenses, and maintaining the proper relationship, i.e., not behaving in a way that could be damaging to their reputation or future earning potential.

Paperwork and records. An employer must also keep good records and paperwork in order to make sound and accurate business decisions. This will help you avoid making errors or omissions when paying staff and keeping track of their entitlements.

Staff health and safety in the workplace. It is an obligation of the employer to provide a safe workplace that employees can feel comfortable working within. It should be free of physical hazards as well as possible issues relating to employee mental health. Employers should aim to reduce the dangers that their employees are exposed to by following the relevant local Occupational Health and Safety guidelines.

Superannuation and taxation. Employers may be obliged to pay superannuation to employees based on their type of employment. Tax regulations must also be followed, as outlined by your local tax regulations.

Anti-discrimination practices. Employers must ensure that the workplace is free from discrimination and any other forms of harassment. All staff must have equal opportunity in the workplace in regards to incentives and promotions. This is important not only from a legal standpoint but to maintain good employee relations.

Dispute resolution. When problems arise in the

workplace, an employer should have a formal, well-documented dispute resolution process in place to deal with the issues in a consistent, fair, and well documented fashion.

Insurance. Certain insurance requirements may be in effect in your region, and you will be required to follow them as an employer.

Step 14: Employee Entitlements

When the time comes for you to take on new employees, you should be aware of all the relevant employee entitlements. These can range from wages and work conditions to holidays, leave, superannuation and redundancy entitlements. Check your local laws and regulations. Here is an example: many jobs in Australia are covered by a federal or state award that outlines the rights and obligations of employers and the minimum legal wage rates and conditions associated with each type of work. These regulations vary from country to country, but in Australia for example, they are outlined by *Fair Work Australia*.

In some workplaces, individuals may be covered by an agreement that sets out specific wages, entitlements and conditions of employment. As an employer, you are often required to grant employees certain leave and holiday entitlements. Most workers are paid for public holidays, except for contract or casual employees who are only paid for hours worked. Other paid leave includes annual or recreational leave, sick leave, and long service leave. Each employee's award or agreement will contain information on their holiday and leave entitlements and the relevant pay arrangements.

There are also regulations regarding maximum hours and limits on the number of consecutive days an employee may be required to work. In other scenarios, regulations may not be in place and workers may be employed on a written contract of employment which sets out specific conditions and entitlements. In some venues, employees are entitled to superannuation payments from their employer. Employees that have been made redundant also have a number of entitlements.

A good approach to employ is to treat your team as you would prefer to be treated: with professionalism, compassion, and kindness; and if you have hired the right people in the first place, you will be repaid many times over by their dedication and commitment to you and your business.

Step 15: The Recruitment Process

If you plan to employ new workers, first determine the type of employees most suitable for the positions you require and the skills and attributes you are looking for in the employees. Our clients use a variety of psychometric benchmarking, testing, and evaluation tools that not only assess a potential team member's IQ but also their EQ (Emotional Intelligence), as well as their integrity and work ethics.

We offer an online or live recruitment training course at:

www.moreprofitlesstime.net

The training addresses recruitment, leadership, developing a winning team, and more with a simple step-by-step process showing you what to do or not do all the while avoiding some of those less than reputable merchants often referred to as "recruitment agencies."

Recruitment Costs

Before you start advertising for additions to your workforce, consider the relevant costs associated with employing new people. It is also a good idea to prepare a *job description* that defines the role, responsibilities, and functions of the new position. This can help you to identify the knowledge, experience, and skill requirements of your future employees.

Once you have prepared a job description, consider how you will advertise the position. There are a number of ways you can do this, including newspapers, internet-based employment sites, or through a local or regional employment agency. It is important to note that when advertising for a position, you are required by law not to use discriminatory language that may exclude potential employees based on race, age, sex, marital status, family status or responsibility, pregnancy, religious and political beliefs, disability, gender history, or sexual orientation.

Have a solid plan for your interview process. Ensure that you ask questions relevant to the job description. Try to assess each candidate based on the quality and honesty of their answers, and notify each of them with an answer as soon as you have made your decision.

The success of your recruiting will rely on your knowledge of the process and how well you:

» Advertise
» Select the right applicants
» Interview
» Document a formal offer of employment

A number of resources are available to assist you and help you develop your knowledge of the recruitment process. We have developed training, support, and tools to help our clients with their recruitment needs. For more information, visit *www.moreprofitlesstime.net*.

Step 16: Legal Requirements

As an employer, you have a number of legal requirements and obligations to adhere to. These are related to awards and conditions, superannuation, compensation and OH&S regulations. It is critical that you have enough knowledge and guidance in this area to comply with your local laws. Remember: there is a reason business lawyers had to study so long to become experts.

Awards and Conditions

Your legal requirements as an employer oblige you to provide a minimum award for your employees and offer certain conditions. In Australia, for example, federal and state legislation is in effect to standardize workplace awards and conditions.

These standards outline minimum requirements for:

» Basic rates of pay and casual loadings
» Maximum hours of work
» Leave entitlements
» Other related entitlements

Superannuation

As an employer, you may have a legal obligation to provide superannuation support to your employees. The purpose of compulsory superannuation is to ensure as many people as possible will have income support when they retire. There are penalties for employers who fail to provide minimum retirement contributions for their employees. Employers who make late contributions may also be obliged to pay penalties to the tax office that enforces these obligations.

Workers' Compensation

In many regions of the world, employers must provide Workers' Compensation insurance for their employees. Workers' compensation provides valuable protection to cover loss of earning capacity, medical expenses, and rehabilitation costs in the event of a work-related accident, illness, or injury. It also provides for expenses associated with assisting employees who are returning to work.

All employers must ensure that they have a Workers' Compensation policy to insure themselves against compensation claims for workplace-related injuries.

Occupational Health and Safety

As an employer, it is a legal requirement that you abide by the occupational health and safety (OH&S) regulations. If you fail to comply with these regulations, you can be liable to prosecution and fines. Personally, I see this not only as an *obligation,* but also as an *opportunity* to ensure that my team goes home safely to their family and loved ones at the end of every day. I encourage you to not just *meet,* but to *exceed* the minimum requirements. One slip-up here can cost a worker's life or result in serious injury. I like being proud of the guy I see in the mirror each day. Your obligations as an employer include ensuring the following:

>> Safe working premises
>> Safe equipment, machinery and substances
>> Safe systems and procedures of work
>> Adequate information, instruction, training, and supervision
>> A suitable working environment and facilities

Equal Employment Opportunity

As an employer, you are required to provide equal employment opportunities to all members of the community. Equal employment opportunity is about ensuring that all job seekers share equal access to work prospects and positions. Without getting carried away with being, "politically correct," you need to ensure that you hire the right people for the right reasons for the right job regardless of their race, gender, sexual or political persuasion and so on. This can be achieved by making sure yor workplace and recruitment processes are free from all forms of unlawful discrimination and harassment.

Check out the online business training information by visiting the following website:

www.moreprofitlesstime.net

Once there, look up the Business Essentials Series Modules 8, 11, and 12. They cover all of the fundamentals you will need to work on before doing anything more in this area. Also included in these training programs are a great DVD, CD, Workbook and various tools to help you.

5   *MARKETING & SALES*

I must admit: this is my favorite subject and one that is too often neglected and or misunderstood by almost every new business owner who doesn't come from a sales and or marketing background. In my early teens, I started off working after school and weekends selling door-to-door home security products, which in the early 1980's was a new market with extremely expensive products, so selling security systems was a difficult prospect but one I excelled at.

I learned early on that if you don't understand people (and what motivates them), you don't understand marketing and sales, so all the gimmicks and clever closes in the world will not help you sell. You must guide people to buy with emotion and give them a logical justification for their purchase. There are no magic bullets here; rather, there are lots of very simple low to no-cost things you can do to maximize your sales and marketing results. Admittedly, to the uninitiated, some of this can appear to be "magic."

I have written a book that addresses this subject in depth, and it will be available soon. For now, just understand that it is important to have at least a general understanding of the basic marketing and selling processes when starting your business. We can build on these fundamental concepts later when you gain proficiency on the subject.

In this chapter, you can find information about conducting market research, market planning, and the goals of selling. Engage these topics before you hire a salesperson or develop sales training programs for your employees.

Step 17: Overview of Marketing

The purpose of marketing is to gain a balance between creating more value for customers and making profits for the organization. Notice that there is a distinction between the activities of "marketing" and plain old "advertising." I use the phrase "creating more value" because marketing includes that while advertising may not. In order to achieve this balance in your business, you first need to understand some of the basic concepts and activities related to marketing.

Marketing Orientation

A marketing orientation involves focusing your business on identifying and understanding your customers' preferences in terms of needs and wants, and delivering them more effectively and efficiently than competitors. Exceed their expectations and they will become your raving fans for life.

Competitive Strategies

Competitive strategies allow businesses to effectively engage their particular environment and successfully compete in the marketplace. Since all business situations are different, there is no single strategy that best fits all organizations. In fact I work with my coaching clients to create at least 10 low and no cost strategies that can be implemented over time and sustained indefinitely. There are quite literally hundreds of low and no cost strategies, so don't be sucked into expensive campaigns that may not offer you a strong return on your investment.

Why 10?

Quite simply, I can answer this by quoting the great Henry Ford. He said, "Only half of your marketing ever works. The problem is I don't know which half." The important thing to remember is that if you underpin your marketing or sales strategies on just one thing you may be setting yourself up for a catastrophic failure. However, there are three types of competitive overarching strategies or ideals that you can adopt depending on your position in the market and particular objectives:

1) *Cost Leadership* – Organizations that follow this strategy aim to provide their products and services at a lower cost than any of their competitors.

2) *Differentiation* – Organizations that follow this strategy concentrate on creating a highly differentiated product line and marketing program in order to become the class leader in their industry.

3) *Focus/Niche* – Organizations that follow this strategy are usually smaller firms that focus their efforts on serving a few market segments effectively rather than dealing with the entire market.

I have seen over the recent years that niches are getting smaller and smaller so my personal favorite is a blend of differentiation and focus/niche. It allows my businesses and those of my clients to be different and stand out in a sea of mediocrity while focusing on a niche where I can be the absolute expert rather than trying to be all things to all people and ending up a master of none.

Marketing Objectives

Marketing objectives define what is to be accomplished

through your marketing activities. When setting objectives, ensure that your objectives are: Specific, Measurable, Achievable, Realistic, and Time-specific.

This gives the appropriate acronym "SMART."

The 'SMART' approach allows you to (1) effectively manage your marketing activities and (2) determine how successful they have been and (3) determine whether they have delivered the particular benefits you seek.

Unique Selling Proposition (USP)

A USP makes your product or service stand out from your competitors and is generally the reason customers purchase your product or service over those of your competitors. Some of the common USPs are "best service," "lowest price," "best value," and "most advanced technology." The aim is to identify these factors and convey them effectively in the marketplace.

If you aren't unique the only thing you can compete on is price and that means discounting which means lower profits which is more often than not a really bad thing.

Who wants to work harder and make less money?

Certainly not me!

We have training and tools to help you identify your USP. These are located in our coaching and training programs.

Market Types

The success of your marketing strategy also depends on you gaining a comprehensive understanding of the particular markets you serve. These markets can either be consumer markets or business markets.

» **Consumer markets** – involve the purchase and sale of goods and services to consumers for their own use rather than for resale.
» **Business markets** – involve sales and purchases of goods and services to various businesses,

governments, and market intermediaries to facilitate the finished product which is generally then re-sold to an end user.

Step 18: Customer & Competitor Research

For your marketing efforts to be successful, you need to understand your market and focus on identifying your consumers, competitors, and the external factors that may influence your business. You may also need to conduct market research to identify trends and perform various types of analysis to identify your business' internal strengths and weaknesses and the external opportunities and threats.

Identifying Customers

Your market may consist of different customers with different buying patterns. Some may prefer impulse purchasing while others may prefer taking their time and getting assistance from others. Getting a good understanding of how consumers think, what their buying habits are and what factors influence these habits is essential for you to make the most of your marketing opportunities.

Identifying Competitors

In simple terms, your competitors can be identified as those companies that offer similar products or services at comparable prices to the same group of customers. These can be either *direct* or *indirect* competitors.

> » **Direct competitors** – These are businesses that sell products or services that are identical or nearly identical to those you sell. For example, Kodak identifies Fuji as a major or direct competitor for camera products.

> » **Indirect competitors** – These are businesses that sell products or services that are similar but not identical to yours. For example, Kodak and Fuji identify Apple

as an indirect competitor because it offers iPhones with digital cameras as an integrated feature.

PEST Analysis

PEST analysis helps you identify and understand the various *environmental factors* that can impact your business and its marketing activities. These include political and legal factors, economic conditions, social and cultural values, and the technological environment in which your business operates. PEST analysis also assists you in adjusting your marketing efforts with external changes that occur over time.

Step 19: Marketing Research & Planning

Marketing research is the process of planning, collecting, and analyzing information related to a marketing decision you must make. Marketing research is vital as it provides you with the specific data you need to break up or segment markets, decide on which areas to target, and identify the best way to position your business relative to your competitors. It can also help you understand trends in the market and can assist you in forecasting future sales and anticipating events and market changes that can impact your business.

SWOT Analysis

SWOT is an acronym for Strengths, Weaknesses, Opportunities, and Threats. A SWOT analysis helps you understand the internal strengths and weaknesses of your business as well as the external opportunities and threats. The goal of a SWOT analysis is to identify the critical factors affecting your organization and then build on your strengths to reduce your weaknesses, exploit opportunities, and avoid the potential threats.

Marketing Planning

Marketing planning starts with deciding on a business

description and involves segmenting your market, targeting the most profitable segments, and positioning your products and services effectively in the marketplace. It also involves choosing the right marketing mix for your business to maximize the effectiveness of your marketing efforts.

Business Description

A business description allows you to get your ideas, plans, and visions down on paper before you go any further. It is important to have a business description as it provides a thorough explanation of what your business is and the direction that you intend it to follow.

Market Segmentation

Market segmentation involves grouping your various customers into segments that have common needs or that will respond similarly to a particular marketing action. Understanding the concept of segmentation is central to marketing because each customer group will require a different marketing mix strategy. You can segment your market based on demographics, psychographics, behavior, or geographical locations.

Targeting

Once you have segmented your market based on different characteristics, choose one or more target market segments. Developing different marketing strategies for different customer groups is very important as no single strategy will satisfy all customer groups since they have differing characteristics, lifestyles, backgrounds and income levels; however, the following are three general strategies for selecting your target markets:

1) *Undifferentiated targeting* – This type of targeting is when you merge your general target market into one big pool and hope something sticks.

2) *Concentrated targeting* – This type of targeting is when you focus on a single niche or specific market. As an example, in my own business, accountants who look after start-up, small, and medium-sized businesses make up my biggest target market. Why? Because they are doing business with the people I want to do business with, and if they trust me to help their clients, their clients will trust me to help them too.

3) *Multi-segment targeting* – This type of targeting allows you to direct your marketing efforts at multiple markets simultaneously and is particularly effective when those different segments have a common thread. For example, I mentioned earlier that my biggest focus is on accountants who service start-up and small to medium-sized businesses. I also focus on franchise groups and industry groups whose memberships are predominantly startups and small to medium-sized businesses.

Prior to selecting a particular targeting strategy, you should perform a Cost Benefit Analysis between all available strategies and then develop a collaborative plan that supports your goals, and budgets.

Positioning

"Positioning" a product or service refers to the act of creating an image or concept in the customer's mind about the product or service or developing a perception of the experience the customer will enjoy by purchasing your product or service. You can positively influence the perceptions of your chosen customer base through strategic promotional activities and by carefully defining the marketing mix of your business.

Marketing Mix

Once you have decided on your overall competitive marketing strategy, you can then focus on planning the details of your marketing mix. A marketing mix is a set of controlled variables that formulate the strategic position of a product or service in the marketplace. The primary goal of marketing is to optimize and offer the best possible combination of the Four P's:

1) Product
2) Price
3) Place
4) Promotion

Then work out the best way to maximize the effectiveness of your marketing efforts. Check out the online training programs we have developed at *www.moreprofitlesstime.net* and look up the Business Essentials Series, Modules 3, 4, 5, 7, 8, 9, 10. They cover all of the fundamentals you will need to work with before you do anything more. The series includes a DVD, CD, Workbook and tools that will help you.

6   *TAKING IT ONLINE*

Since the mid-1990s, the business world has undergone a massive transition from offline to online, and most companies now have some form of online presence. If your new business does not have a good online footprint—and more importantly does not embrace the available tools—then you will slowly be left behind by the competition. There are simply too many Internet-based automation and communication tools to ignore. Some old-timers have still not fully accepted the online experience as a valid business platform, but you will need to embrace—in some fashion—the online world if you want to succeed in your new business.

This section deals with the prominent topics you need to understand to ensure that your new business remains competitive and prospers in this rapidly evolving landscape—or should I refer to it as the rapidly evolving cyberscape? I think so.

I do not present an exhaustive treatment of online marketing in this book; rather, I present the main concepts, especially those you must understand to launch your company and compete effectively in this increasingly online world. In order to give you a good foundation, I will get a little bit technical, but I think this area is so important that I want you to spend the time necessary to read this section closely (maybe twice) so you can make the important decisions with respect to online marketing and transacting your business online.

Step 20: Your Online Presence

Almost everything you do online will fall into two main categories:

1) Online Marketing
2) Transacting Business Online

The first has to deal with advertising and your online footprint; the second category relates to those automation tools you will use to facilitate your daily transactions (for example, email). Since so many things in the offline world are being (have been) replaced by an online counterpart, you will need to have an online presence and the sooner the better. You do not necessarily have to create an extravagant website *before* you start operating your business. You can build it after you are up and running if you want, but it is a very good idea to understand what you will need at the outset. If you are asking yourself the question, *Should I start my business offline first or develop the online footprint before I start my business?*

Think of it this way: In a sense, we have the proverbial "chicken-and-egg" situation here, and I don't want you to spend so much time and money designing and creating your online presence (the chicken) that your new business (the egg) never has a chance to hatch!

Sometimes it is better to get any bugs out of your new business before you create the online counterpart. You can develop your online presence (website and online business automation) as you go. You will want to do some things from the get-go, one of those being online marketing.

Online Marketing Techniques

Some online marketing techniques parallel the traditional offline techniques, so they are easier to understand. For example, email marketing is very similar to traditional postal service marketing. You have mailing lists in both realms and you send messages and run promotions in both realms. There are differences, but the concept is similar.

Other forms of online marketing do not have such clear counterparts in the real world. They are less intuitive in nature and therefore more difficult to understand. For example, pay-per-click advertising. In the online world this activity refers to a type of advertising where the advertiser pays each time a prospect clicks on the advertisement and is transported to the target webpage. This would be comparable to advertising on a road sign and then each time a prospect read that advertisement and contacted your business (as a result of reading it), you would pay the owner of the sign for advertising. This might be a good way to advertise and many businesses would probably agree to pay for each prospect arriving at the door in this fashion, but in the offline world it is simply not possible to accurately track such leads. Many businesses ask a client where they heard about the business, and some businesses do give rewards for delivering new customers, but it is just not as feasible in the offline world as it is in the online world. Everything is tracked online, so it is much easier to manage. When a prospect clicks a link online and then is delivered to a business website, that business can instantly determine who sent them there and pay a resulting commission. Thus you have pay-per-click (affiliate marketing is also based on this).

In addition to determining where website traffic originates, you can also track everything a customer does when they visit your website: which pages they go to, how much time they spend in a certain area, and every time they click their mouse button, and on what they click. This provides a tremendous amount of vital data you can use in your marketing efforts.

Let me give you one big reason to have an online presence with your business, and nobody can argue with this: people are increasingly using online search tools to find the services and products they need. It's a fact that landline telephone systems are being phased out; replacing this traditional communication platform are cell phones, tablet computers, and laptops. While in 1995, almost everyone used some type of telephone directory—mostly in hardcopy format—to locate the contact information for a business, in 2014 almost no one does. The old telephone book directory has gone the way of the newspaper classified section (or the dinosaur)—most of it is now done online. The bottom line: if you want your prospects to find you, you must get online, and if you fail to do so at the outset, your new business will suffer from the get-go.

Backlink Generation

Backlinks are probably the most important concept in online marketing, so you should understand them first. Simply put, backlinks are the links on a webpage that when clicked, take you to another place on the Internet. Here is the key concept with backlinks: Goggle search is driven mostly by backlinks, and to get a higher position in the search results, you need to have "quality" backlinks that point to your website.

For example, the developers of Google created their search engine with the goal of providing relevant search results. In their 2004 prospectus, they stated their mission as:

"To organize the world's information and make it universally accessible and useful."

In order to accomplish this mission, every few weeks Google runs a program that "spiders" the entire Internet (this means they visit each webpage, assigning a rank or number to each webpage. This is a complicated way of saying that they look at all the webpages and rank each page according to several factors, one being the number of other pages that link to it. If a lot of webpages on the Internet link to your site, your site will appear higher in the search results, and usually this translates to more business. Simply put, Google believes that if many websites link to your site, then your site must be more important. More weight (meaning a higher ranking) is given to your webpage if a webpage that points to yours has a high pagerank itself. So backlinks have more power to rank you higher if they are located on a higher ranking site. The number of backlinks you have is not the only thing that determines your ranking. Many other factors come into play. One example is the quality score of your website.

So what do most savvy Internet marketers spend their time doing?

Building backlinks. They want their money site to appear higher in the search rankings, so they build quality backlinks to increase their traffic and get more conversions. In the online marketing world, everything depends on backlinks.

But there is one thing about backlinks that you need to understand: you cannot just go around the Internet posting links to your website; you need to have content associated with those backlinks. And the higher the quality of that content, the higher your site will appear in the search results. You cannot generate pages and pages of random text that contains links to your webpage. The search engines are smarter than that and they will realize what you are up to and actually lower your ranking as a result.

In the early days, enterprising online marketers did just that: they tricked the search engines by creating thousands of keywords that were invisible to the eye because they were displayed in a font with the same color as the background of the webpage; this made the page seem more important because of all the keywords. To illustrate, suppose a website sold plumbing parts. The web programmer would build a page with thousands of words about plumbing that actually made no sense if read by a visitor (remember, visitors could not see it because of the font color), but the search engines then were very primitive and surmised that any webpage with so many words about plumbing must be a good site for people who were searching for plumbing parts and that site was assigned a high score based on this faulty logic. Even so, the owners of that site sold more parts. As the search engines grew smarter, they disallowed these types of "tricks." The online marketers then did other things to get higher rankings and the search engines adjusted again.

I am relating this story because it illustrates very well the ongoing relationship between online marketers and the search engines. It is very much like a cat and mouse game with both sides constantly evolving and adapting to changes by the other. You will need to understand this game, or at least have a good business coach on your side who can help you navigate this turbulent sea of online marketing.

In essence, the search engines simply try to determine the best sites to return when a searcher types words into the search box. To do so they must first go out and gather information about the many available websites. This is where the spidering process comes into play. The result of that process is to assign every webpage a score based on the keywords found on that page and the related backlinks, and when a searcher types those keywords into the search box, those webpages with the highest score appear at the top of the search results. The searcher clicks on those links, and then is transported to the webpage and conceivably buys products and services from the owner of that website.

This is how it works in the simplest form, but as with

everything else, it is much more complicated than this; other factors come into play, such as the quality of your website content and the different types of content your backlinks are associated with. During the spidering process, the search engine considers the various types of content you make available on your website in addition to the external backlinks to your site. Here is a partial list of the possible content types where backlinks can exist:

Blogs	Social Media	Articles
Online Newsletters	EBooks	Videos
White Papers	Presentations	Case Studies
Webinars	Infographics	Branded Content
Ezines	Mobile Content	Microsites
Mobile Apps	Podcasts	Syndicated Content
Press Releases	Annual Reports	Online Forums

So if you want to be higher in the search rankings, one way to do it is to generate the above content forms for placement on your own website and or on other websites as well; inside this content, or around it, you place backlinks to your website.

Article Marketing

I will illustrate these concepts—and how you can improve your online search ranking—by showing you how you can use articles to increase your backlinks. In the early days of article marketing (not so long ago—about 2005), you could use the concept of article marketing, in its most primitive form, to get your site to the very top of the search results page in your niche. Several people discovered they could write a high volume of short articles (about 250 words in length) on topics related to their niche, and then place these articles at strategic locations on the Internet to get to the very top of the search results page. Their sales increased dramatically and they made a tremendous amount of money—even though they only had a small (prior to all the newfound success) business operation, possibly even an entirely home-based business run just by themselves. Some people made millions of dollars from article marketing.

Various companies arose to accommodate the placement of these articles. These companies simply allowed article writers to post articles on their websites so the articles had a home on the Internet. The search engines then spidered the articles and found the backlinks to the website of the article author. The best articles were SEO-optimized (more on that in the next section), and each article dealt with one facet of the niche in which the author sold products. For example, if you sold debt reduction services, you could write an article on "Improving Your Credit Score" or one on "Negotiating with Collection Agencies" and so forth, with each article containing biographical information about your business and links to your website. If you sold almost any product, you could generate articles about your product and increase the number of backlinks to your website with article marketing.

Enterprising entrepreneurs soon discovered that they could hire article writers to write large amounts of articles and increase their backlinks even more. Software developers wrote software that would generate five articles from a single article. This increased the volume of backlinks even more. Software was also available to distribute large amounts of articles in an automated fashion, so you could author your article and click a button to have it uploaded to hundreds of online article repositories. Soon, it was possible for a single person to generate and distribute literally hundreds or thousands of "unique" articles throughout the Internet, all with backlinks to their money site. Those who generated articles in this fashion directed large amounts of Internet traffic to their site after they appeared at the top of the search results, and they became very rich.

A year or so after the word got out, so many people were using article marketing to increase their search ranking that the search engines (more accurately, the people who *control* the search engines) put a stop to it, sort of. They added logic into the spidering algorithm such that these massive blasts of cheesy articles no longer had the desired effect, and in some cases—such as when an article was duplicated in multiple online locations—the site being backlinked was put lower in the rankings. In essence, the search engine said "No! We will no longer allow you to put all that low quality content on the Internet to increase your rankings in a roundabout way."

Understand that these article marketers were just doing what worked. This activity would be comparable to placing thousands of road signs along the highway. Eventually, the highway gets so cluttered with cheap signage that it becomes distracting to the drivers and the government steps in and passes laws to prevent all the cheesiness (for lack of a better word). In this case, the government would be those individuals who control the search engines.

What is the state of article marketing now?

You can still do it, but you won't get as much value from using software and other means to generate large amounts of low quality articles. You can still gain value by generating some high-quality article content; you just can't go overboard with the short, high-volume articles or it will be a detriment to your efforts. If you want to spend the money to hire good writers to generate high-quality articles, you can get yourself higher in the rankings.

I am telling you about article marketing, and spending a little more time on it, because it is a simple way to illustrate that you can take actions to scale your content development and gain a positive effect on your ranking in the search results. Article marketing is representative of most of the things happening in online marketing, so it is critical that you understand it. Most importantly, online marketing is becoming so critical that you simply cannot ignore it any longer.

If you get the right business coach to help you, and you have some money to fund your efforts, you can get to the very top of the search rankings, and it is still not as difficult as you might think (as long as you don't try to do it with a million cheesy articles). Article marketing is still one of many ways to play the online marketing game. As you can see from the list of content forms in the previous section, in addition to article marketing, you can and should use many other forms of content to increase your search rankings, and the search algorithms are not as sophisticated with some of these alternatives as they are with articles. Whatever you do in the online marketing realm, you will need to have at least a basic understanding of Search Engine Optimization (SEO), so I will talk about that next.

SEO

SEO is an acronym for *Search Engine Optimization,* and it refers to the act of optimizing your online content to best meet the expectations of the search engines. In other words, you structure your content such that it gets you the highest ranking in the search results for the keywords in your niche. If you are selling a certain product, that product has certain keywords and phrases associated with it, and you need to structure your content so it presents those keywords and phrases in the right proportion to the other words in your content piece.

Google – The Gold Standard in Search

Now that we are on this topic, I will point out that there is really only one search engine (that matters), and that is Google. Google is the gold standard in the search game since they control about 80% of the search market. Yahoo is next with about 10%, followed by Bing. Most SEO efforts and standards are based on what the Google pagerank algorithm expects to find. If that algorithm assigns a higher score to debt reduction articles that use the word "debt" at a certain rate in proportion to the content, then SEO experts strive to achieve that exact proportion in all the content they generate.

How do the SEO experts know the correct proportions?

They use a lot of trial and error, but Google also has tools available to assist you with optimizing your content. The functionality of these tools falls outside the scope of this book, but you should be aware that Google does make an effort to help online marketers, and the person you hire to help you should be well versed on the various tools Google makes available in this area.

To illustrate the concept of optimizing your content, consider the extreme case. If you sell debt reduction services, one of the top keywords would obviously be "debt" and a common phrase would be "debt reduction." Although you could structure your article (it does not have to be an article, by the way—it can be any of the content forms listed in the previous section) such that "debt reduction" appears in every single sentence, this is not the best way to do it. The article will not be appealing to the reader and the search engines will assign it a score lower than a piece with a more natural proportion of keywords to content. As I mentioned above, my objective here is not to teach you how to write the very best SEO content; rather, I want to educate you in the process so you can understand it enough to run your new business and work with those experts who will help you with online marketing. You will need to understand these concepts at a basic level to make sales and marketing decisions. You don't have to be the person writing the articles or even managing those who are doing it. That is what your coach and employees are for. You do need to understand how it works so you can communicate with these experts and make strategic decisions for your business. The more you understand, the better your new business will perform.

List Building/Management

In the online world, a list of email addresses—used for email marketing campaigns—is referred to as a "List." Many companies send out weekly or monthly email campaigns, also known as "email blasts," to the addresses in their List. Some aggressive marketers send out *daily* email messages. I do not recommend daily email blasts to your List because they can become quite distracting and you can actually damage the relationship with your client/prospect. The frequency would be a function of the perceived value of the communication. If your prospect finds these communications highly valuable, then you might send more. That will be a decision you need to make.

Whatever you decide, there are some rules to follow when performing email marketing activities. Here is a little bit of history first. Up until about 2003, there were no regulations on email marketing and as the Internet evolved, the amount of marketing emails skyrocketed to the point that so many marketing messages were being generated and sent around that email systems were nearly unusable. Some people had to traverse through pages and pages of marketing emails just to find their non-marketing messages. The governments of the world stepped in and passed legislation to control unsolicited emails, which are also called "SPAM." In Australia, they passed the Spam Act 2003, and in America, they passed the CAN-SPAM Act. These are similar in that they are designed to decrease the overall amount of SPAM on the Internet.

At first, after the regulations were put into effect, they were largely ignored. Then some violators were brought to justice and given severe prison terms for sending SPAM messages. Immediately there was a dramatic decrease in the amount of SPAM. I will not outline all of the regulations here; rather I will give you an overview of the online marketing topics you need to know about to get your business going. You can get the details on those regulations by searching on the act in your country, or check with your attorney or business coach.

The general thing to understand is that you cannot take a list of email addresses and start blasting messages out to people on the list. The regulations require that you include an easy way for the recipient to "opt out" of the list. There are also requirements about the identifying information you must include in the communication. You should not be the person who manages the email campaigns until you have a good understanding of the regulations and the process. Until you do, consult your business coach for guidance.

You should however start building your List when you start your business. You will likely have some type of website, however simple, right from the get-go, and a standard component of any website is the "Contact Us" page. You may or may not have the ability to automate the process of storing the email addresses of prospects who contact you through that interface. In any case, keep a record of those email addresses from the beginning. Save the names and other information also. This data can ultimately be converted into your online marketing List. You can do that early on or accomplish it as your business grows and evolves. At some point, you should send periodic email communications to these people on your List.

Attraction Marketing Concepts

The idea of *Attraction Marketing* is fundamental to online marketing, and it is important that you understand it. Here's why: if you understand Attraction Marketing, you will have all the knowledge you need to build a marketing strategy around any type of online content. The same fundamental concept applies to email marketing, article marketing, and all the various forms (see the list of content types in the *Backlink Generation* section above). The idea spans all of online marketing.

Attraction Marketing refers to the process of branding yourself as an expert using various forms of content. Here's how it works: Although you sell a simple, low-cost product on your website (or you give it away for free) and most of your content is aimed at selling that product (or products), you also sell a larger more expensive product, one that generates the main profits for your company.

To illustrate this idea in simple fashion, consider a niche in the computer field: *computer security*. Suppose you are a security expert and you want to go into business as a consultant. You could simply advertise yourself as an expert and hope to land clients, or you could use another approach: you could give a low-cost seminar on the topic of computer security. At that seminar, you are likely to meet clients who will pay you a lot of money over the years to help manage their computer security issues. Although you did not make much revenue on the seminar fee, you did make a lot on the followup consulting fees. You could also write a book about computer security. You may not make a lot of money on the book royalties, but you will from the readers who eventually hire you as a consultant to work on their computer systems.

I would imagine you are familiar with this marketing pattern' you have seen it before, or even used it. Now this is how it works in the online world. You use the various types of online marketing content to brand yourself as an expert, and while selling (or giving away) lower cost products in your niche, you generate leads to clients who will pay you more money for your higher-priced services. If you are a security consultant, you write a software program that provides security, and then you sell that software and manage a support forum where you interact with the users of that software. You also publish various, low-cost how-to guides on security. You distribute a periodic e-newsletter that contains security articles from industry experts, along with a commentary piece you write for every issue.

What is the net effect?

You gain credibility and are perceived as the go-to person in computer security. You then get consulting gigs and you make a comfortable living from the consulting fees.

Do you employ a hard-sell approach with your consulting services?

No.

And that's the most intelligent thing you can do because people prefer not to be *sold to* in a heavy-handed way when the product is high-priced. The want to make up their own minds and with an Attraction Marketing approach you are letting them. As mentioned above, the online concept of Attraction Marketing also has a counterpart in the real world, although it is much more expensive to employ. All the automation tools and facilities that exist online allow you to brand yourself as an expert more easily, and the process is far less expensive. In the real world, you might have to travel around the country— or the world—giving seminars on computer security; in the online world, you can give webinars and generate quality content and facilities that brand you as an expert. The online version is gaining credibility every day. More people trust the online venues, so it is critical that you consider these opportunities at the outset of your business venture. It may be the difference between success and failure since this is far less expensive to accomplish online, and if you do it smartly, with the help of a competent business coach, you can realize immense gains and do it all within your limited budget.

Social Media

The term "Social Media" refers to online services that provide a platform for social networking or engaging with a network of people. These sites provide you with various functions to facilitate your communication with others. They allow you to build a "network" of people and "connect" with others that share common interests. In business, you can make a connection to a potential client through your network using these sites. Again, as with the other topics in this book, I will not offer you an exhaustive how-to on these sites; rather, I will give you enough solid information you can use to get your business started and make the right decisions.

LinkedIn and *Facebook* are two popular social networking sites. They both allow you to create a network of other users to communicate with. You can post and share content; you can use chat and other messaging functions to communicate with those in your network. For business, LinkedIn is the choice because it is tailored for business and people expect you to use it for business reasons rather than personal. Using Facebook for business is not as straightforward. This is primarily because many people use Facebook for personal reasons rather than business. The Facebook company would like you to use it for business and they promote various business-type features, but the reality is that it has evolved as more of a non-commercial-use site, so people can get a little bit offended if they are trying to "connect" with you personally and you respond by pitching them a product or service. Your old girlfriend from high school asks you if you would like to meet for coffee to laugh about old times, and you respond by pitching her some hairspray products? I think you get the idea.

However, with that being said, Facebook lets you run advertising campaigns, and many businesses use this feature.

You can design block ads and pay a certain amount per click. When a prospect clicks on your ad, you then will be charged against a prepaid amount you have put on deposit. The more clicks you get, the less you pay per click. You have probably noticed those businesses who offer enticements to potential customers to "Like" their Facebook page; there is probably an ad campaign going on behind those activities. As I mentioned, Facebook does provide the facilities to run ad campaigns, but you may be offering products and services to some of the "friends" in your network. That is the nature of Facebook. You can set up a Facebook page for your business using your branding. Then you can use it for business reasons and not personal; post announcements there. It is another way to get the word out about happenings in your company.

LinkedIn on the other hand is geared to making *business* connections, and it was designed specifically for that, so people will not be offended as easily when you market to them there. However, a lot of people are marketing their products and services on LinkedIn (basically everyone), so there is a lot more marketing activity and many more distractions. Everyone seems to have some kind of angle on LinkedIn. Your primary and secondary networks can be very powerful lead generation mechanisms, so you should set up an account there as well.

Twitter is another social media venue you can use to get the word out about your business. The primary difference between Twitter and the other social network sites is that when you "tweet" something, like a new product announcement or a press release headline, it goes out immediately to all the individuals in your network. On the other social networking sites, you would post something and they would see it when they logged on. This is not exactly true if they use a cell phone or other live device connected to their account—in which case they may get immediate notification—but close.

So many technologies overlap these days.

The Twitter market would be more of a mix between business and personal use, although it seems a bit more business oriented, possibly a result of all the social media marketers that have developed countless systems and methods of marketing on the social media sites. Again, you don't need to be an expert on all the facets of social networking sites, and I certainly don't want you to spend so much time there that it detracts from running your new business; rather, get a fundamental understanding of these different venues and what they offer. As with other topics, please consult with your business coach to find out how best to leverage these social networking sites.

Pay-Per-Click Versus Pay-Per-View Marketing

The basic difference between these two marketing methods is that you are either paying when someone *clicks on* your advertisement or when they *view* your advertisement. I will give you an example of each.

Pay-Per-Click

With Pay-Per-Click (PPC), you would pay each time a prospect clicks on the backlink and they are directed to your website. You are not guaranteed a sales conversion, just that someone clicked on the ad. I mentioned that Facebook offers PPC advertising. Google AdWords is another popular service offering it. Here is how it works there. Suppose you decide to pay $20 per day on PPC advertising with AdWords. You specify this limit and you can change it any time. You also specify (via a bid in an online auction system) how much you will pay for each click based on the keywords you chose. This amount determines how high your ad will appear in the search results. You have probably noticed that when you search with Google, there are some items at the top of the results page: those are paid advertisements. One problem with PPC advertising is that the prices for good keywords can be high, so your ad does not get prominence unless you are willing to pay a lot.

Pay-Per-View

Pay-Per-View (PPV) advertising uses a different model. Basically, potential clients agree to view advertisements in return for a reduced rate on a product or service. For example, Amazon offers a version of their popular Kindle book reader that displays advertisements with the content you are reading. You can buy this version of the book reader cheaper than the version that does not display ads on the side of the screen. Generally speaking, with PPV advertising, whether a client clicks on the ad or not you pay each time your ad is displayed. Another popular place for PPV advertising is with gaming communities. To give you an idea of the potential lead pool, consider TrafficVance, a company that offers PPV services. They deliver over 350 million target impressions per month. As an advertiser, you can target specific keywords and phrases. TrafficVance then highlights these keywords and phrases in the online content when a member of their user base browses the Internet, turning them into clickable ads. Game players get a discount in the game environment in return for viewing the advertisements.

The Importance of a Great Website

You know what they say about first impressions: "You don't get a second chance to make one." And when it comes to websites, this couldn't be truer. If you offer any type of service that requires expert workmanship—and most services do—probably the worst thing you can do is present potential clients with a broken website on their first visit. It is safe to conclude that if the website doesn't work, then your service or the product may not work either. The very last thing you want to do is have a website with broken links or something that is off kilter when someone visits. If something is not right with your website, and you leave it that way, it sends the following message about your customer service: If we sell you a product or service and it breaks, we will leave it broken, *just like our website.* Conversely, if everything works perfectly and the user interface is easy to interact with, you are sending the unspoken signal that your products and services will be seamless and of higher quality.

If your website is ugly and the user interface is difficult to use, or it crashes when certain pages are called up, this also implies that what you deliver—product or service—might also be ugly and will not work as advertised. Websites are sort of like people in this way. If a person is dressed poorly and shows up late consistently, it reflects badly on the character of that person. I don't need to go on and on; you get the picture. The important thing here is that you need to be careful about how you design your online presence, which is mostly your website. Your online marketing activities also define your image, but not nearly as much as your company website. For these reasons, it is imperative that you provide a website the (1) works and (2) is pleasing to the eye.

Is your website static and primarily informational, or does it engage the visitor?

Sometimes you want a simple website that is primarily informational, so there are no hard set rules here. You could offer a visitor an enticement such as a free download in return for an email address to be used for marketing products and services later. If you offer subscription-based content on your website, you could let users set up a trial account for some period of time. They could try your service free before becoming a paying subscriber.

You might offer a blog with loads of valuable content and the ability for visitors or subscribers to "ask the expert" questions. Some legal sites do well with this type of structure, but there are also a few very popular horticulture sites and do-it-yourself sites with highly informational forums where experts regularly answer questions posed by visitors. You can offer these types of facilities on your website. If you read the section on Attraction Marketing, you will realize immediately that this is exactly what you need to do in that marketing model. It all depends on the amount of resources you want to put into something like this, and this in turn depends on your niche.

At a minimum, you simply MUST have an attractive website that works and does not have dead hyperlinks. You also need a website that is easy to maintain. Probably the last thing you need for your new business is to develop a very complex website that requires a highly skilled programmer to make simple changes. It would be very costly.

WordPress Websites

Consider building your website on a WordPress platform. This is a popular website platform that makes it easier to develop a high quality website interface with minimal effort. Using WordPress is much easier than building the site from scratch with basic HTML code. Many people are trained in WordPress and there are many templates you can buy at a small cost (less than $100). These templates get you a basic framework you can then tailor to your own needs. Don't get me wrong: building websites—even with WordPress—is not easy and you need a qualified webmaster to help you. Check with your business coach for direction on this.

Another good feature of WordPress is that all WordPress sites use a common user interface, so if you learn how to use that interface, the skill will be valuable elsewhere. WordPress is also designed so non-webmasters can make simple changes and perform periodic maintenance. WordPress also allows for easy backup and recovery and version upgrades. It is very simple to change the overall look and feel of a WordPress site that is filled with your content—not so for a coded, non-Word-Press website.

Here is proof that building websites is not an easy venture: every now and then a company advertises on TV or somewhere else that they have made website creation as simple as clockwork. They present an interface in the advertisement that shows how easy it is to set up and maintain your website with their product. Yet to date, there has been no company that has emerged as being the go-to company for easy, cost-effective website creation and management. All of them seem to fade out of the limelight. If creating websites was such an easy process, there would be a Google of website creation, or a Facebook, or an Amazon—some type of industry leader in website creation. A big company would have solved it and they would be the obvious leader, yet notice that no company has accomplished this. I point this out so you know that website creation is not simple and you will need help with it. Do not hire a fly-by-night outfit to build your website on a questionable hosting service. The future of your new business may be severely impacted by such a decision. Get good solid advice from your business coach about how best to proceed with your online presence.

Hosting Services

I will be talking a little more in depth about affiliate marketing soon, but I will mention it here as it relates to websites. Affiliate marketing is a form of marketing where a company will pay their affiliates for delivering paid customers to their service. Here is where it relates to websites. When you purchase your website, you will basically get two things:

1) A hosting account
2) The code that comprises your website

The hosting account is the *place* where the website code will exist. It is like an empty storage device. When you put the code onto the hosting account, the website comes alive. You cannot have a website without having both of these components. You will pay some amount periodically for the hosting account fees, but you will pay only once for the setup of the website (and then each time you make changes). Affiliate marketing comes into play here because some hosting services offer their affiliates kickbacks when they deliver customers to the hosting service. Some website developers use these hosting services because after they set up the website, they continue to earn revenue every time the client renews the subscription to the hosting service. This can be a bad deal for you because these hosting servers are often more costly since they need to charge more so they can pay the affiliates. Another gotcha is the interface for web development and the domain service. Without getting too technical, some of these affiliate-based hosting services make it more difficult for you to terminate your hosting subscription and move somewhere else. It is better to find a web developer that is not getting any kickbacks from the hosting service they are building your website on. Keep these two things separate and you have a better chance of avoiding costly conflicts in the future.

In summary, I would recommend that you start with a WordPress platform and go with a hosting service that is not affiliated too closely with the developer of your website. Build a simple site at the outset and let the complexity of your website evolve with your business as it grows.

Cloud Computing

In this section, I discuss some data processing topics with respect to *cloud computing*, but this discussion on these topics will also inform you about many critical concepts in general computing—concepts you need to run your new business. From the time you launch your company, you should understand things like data security, system backup, software reliability, and support. I will talk about these things with respect to cloud computing, and in doing so give you a general presentation on these highly critical topics.

You have surely heard the term "cloud computing." In general it relates to the idea of sharing resources in a "cloud," a jargon term for the Internet or some kind of network. You may have also heard of Gmail. Gmail exists online so it is essentially a cloud-based service. I am going to use it as an example because it exemplifies all the pros and cons of using cloud-based services for your business. Similar arguments *for* and *against* can be made with most cloud-based services.

Since you are going into business for yourself, it is very important that you understand what the cloud is, and the pros and cons of using services based in the cloud. These services can save you a lot of money, and remember: Cash-flow is king! If you keep more money in your own pocket, your-cash flow will be much healthier. The basic idea here is that you will need several data processing functions in your business— word processing, accounting, email, spreadsheet, presenta- tions, and others—and you can use cloud-based software for these functions or you can purchase them and manage them yourself (usually at a higher cost).

For example, you will need to use email in your new business and you have several configuration choices to pick from when you make your decision on which email program to use. Here are some considerations, and these will span all such services:

> » *Security* – How secure is your email system and the communications to and from your business?
> » *Backup & Recovery* – If you lose some email data, can you get another copy?
> » *Cost* – How much does the email service cost?
> » *Reliability* – What is the reliability of the email service?

» *Functionality* – Does the email service have all the functions you need for your business?

Security

Your company emails should be secure and private. Business information has value and keeping it private can make the difference between success and failure. If you develop a proprietary system that you are selling, developing that system had a cost associated with it, and you do not want to just give that system away to a competitor because then the competitor will be able to use your system to deliver the same service. Since such services are usually priced to include the research and development in the price, your competitor would then be able to charge a lower price for the same service since they spent nothing on research and development. You can see the problem. If someone—a competitor—can access all of your emails, they will have access to a tremendous amount of the proprietary data owned by your company. If you use a service like Gmail, in the cloud and unsecured, you will be compromising your business on security. Gmail is based on the fact that all of your email remains unencrypted so that the Gmail software can parse the text of your email and add targeted advertisements based on content. While Gmail representatives claim that no one—no real person—actually looks at your emails, you cannot be guaranteed of that. In reality, most such systems are open to the eyes of many people (system administrators, support personnel, nosey relatives, and others). Conceivably, your emails (and all the attachments you send with them) could be viewed by anyone at all if you use an unsecured, cloud-based service like Gmail.

Another option would be to host your own email server. This would be more expensive because you would need to set it up and manage it, but it would offer you more security—and thus the proprietary information of your new company would be secure. The most secure solution would be to subscribe to a web-based service that offers full encryption.

You may not be concerned with having encryption and strong security in the initial phases of your start-up. If you are not, a cloud-based service like Gmail may work for you in the short-term because it is simple to get started on, free, and it has many good features. If you wish to get an email service that offers more security and other features, you should work with your business coach to get the email program you desire.

Backup & Recovery

This is probably one of the most overlooked areas in business computing. A very high percentage of companies do not have an adequate backup and recovery plan in place. Typically, the problem starts with a sub-standard method of archiving company transaction data. Most businesses fail to realize that they are not storing their critical data on backup until a disaster occurs and they need that data—and it is not there. This can be a very costly mistake. If you lose some emails, it will be very difficult to contact Google and get them to provide you with a copy of all the emails you lost. You may be able to do it, but since you get the service free, Google does not guarantee they will respond to you, or that they are even backing up your email data.

However, and this goes for many cloud-based services, with respect to general backup and recovery of other critical company data, there are some good cloud-based solutions. I am not talking just about emails here; rather, I am referring to all the critical data of your company, the accounting history, contracts, daily transactions, database information, etc. This data also needs to be backed up, and a cloud-based solution that offers local encryption is likely a lot more reliable and cost-effective than what you can do locally if you set up your own backup system. You should pay for this service so the usual drawbacks associated with free cloud services like Gmail are not present. Also make sure your data is secure.

Cost

Gmail is completely free, but as mentioned above, if you need support, you might as well wish into the wind because when you dial the Google phone number (if you can even find it), I doubt anyone will answer. I cannot say for certain this is true with Google, but it is generally the case with all of the *free* cloud-based services. Skype would be another example. You can use their free facilities, but there is very little live support. If you want a support phone number for a cloud service, you will likely need to pay a subscription fee.

Reliability

Gmail is very reliable, as are most of the larger cloud-based systems. Usually they are much more reliable than what you can provide yourself if you host a solution in-house. These cloud services are hosted in multi-geographical regions, meaning that if one of their servers goes down for any reason, another server picks up service instantaneously. It would be very expensive to provide this level of system availability and redundancy in-house. In this respect, cloud-based services are the system of choice, especially for business startups.

Functionality

You will generally get better functionality from a non-cloud service, but subscription-based cloud services (those you pay for) will provide better functionality than the free ones, and here's why: if you are paying a company to use their software, they will generally be more responsive to your individual needs and requests. You will not have much hope of getting Google to make a change in their Gmail program to meet one of your internal company needs; you will, however, have better luck if you buy an email program, or subscribe to one. In the latter case, the vendor is making their revenue from you *directly*, so they need to keep you happy. Google does not care as much about the functionality you need for your particular business, and they are using you to generate revenue *indirectly*. In summary, you tend to get better functionality for services that you pay for. This is not true in every instance, but it is generally the case.

Common Cloud Tools

There are many cloud-based tools you can take advantage of to get your new business started. As mentioned above, some critical functions—like backup and recovery—can be done very economically with a cloud solution. I will present some of the more popular cloud-based functions here to help you get started. Your new business will have its own unique needs, so check with your business coach for guidance in this area.

Communication – I will list the industry leader here: Skype. They offer online chat, messaging, video conferencing, and other services. Their offerings are extensive, with some free cloud services and some subscription-based.

List Management – These would be vendors of online email marketing services. As outlined above in the email marketing section, your business will eventually have a marketing List and you will likely be doing periodic email blasts to your List. Several such services exist in the cloud. I won't list them all here as you can easily find the leaders online or get the top names from your business coach.

Customer Relationship Management (CRM) System – I am going to tell you the general features of CRM systems and leave it up to your business coach to help you decide which is best. A CRM system allows you to manage your clients. This is a must-have for sales people who need to track leads and follow all the developments in a client relationship, especially if it spans any length of time. If you have more than five clients, you should have some type of CRM system. It will allow you to store account history on a client so that anyone in your company can go back and view what has occurred.

Payment Processing – The industry leader is PayPal, and if you are transacting business online, you will need a PayPal account. Many clients are likely to show up with a PayPal payment for your products and services. PayPal does not replace your local bank, but they do give you a viable alternative to having your global customers send you checks in the mail. If you accept a PayPal payment from a client today, you can have the money in your bank account in a few days. You will have to pay a processing fee, around 4-5% for international transactions, but it makes processing payments much easier for non-local business transactions.

Accounting – As with the other tools, having a cloud-based accounting system will give you the flexibility of allowing multiple people access to it from multiple locations. Your accounting department can be geographically dispersed if need be. The cost for a cloud-based accounting system will be lower on a monthly basis, usually less than 20 USD. Conversely, if you purchase a package to install on your local computer, it can cost hundreds of dollars. Depending on the complexity of your accounting needs, one option may be advantageous over another. Your accountant would probably prefer that you run on a cloud-based system because it makes access easier for them. On a hosted system, you would need to write your accounting data out to disk and deliver the disk to your accountant. It is easier if they can just access your system online; it does, however, bring up the issue of security again. An online accounting system is far less secure: if your accountant can log in from his office, a hacker could also gain access to your vital data and cause you trouble. Your data will be safer physically if it resides in a cloud-based accounting system because a burglary in your office, and the loss of a computer, will not affect the cloud-based system records.

Document Processing – If your workforce is distributed at all, you can solve many problems by using a cloud-based document management and processing program. You will be sharing documents, so having them in a central location— available to everyone—is paramount. If the software you use to edit those documents is also cloud-based, then you do not need to have individual copies on every PC in the workforce. Workers can log on and process the documents online, from anywhere. Collaboration (as with most cloud applications) is easy.

Affiliate Marketing

Affiliate marketing refers to the concept of selling your products and services with the help of "affiliates," or people who are referring customers to you. When someone (an affiliate) sends a prospect your way, and that prospect ends up purchasing a product or service from you, you are obligated to compensate that affiliate. This is not unlike the offline version, which is to pay a commission to distributors who market and sell your products and services.

On the web, affiliate marketing works as follows. You create an affiliate program for your business. On your website, you take applications. Potential affiliates apply to become an affiliate. You approve them and give them backlinks to the purchasing pages of your products and services. Each link contains an affiliate identification code. The affiliate puts advertisements on the Internet (on their website or elsewhere) with links to your products. When someone in the world clicks on an affiliate link, bringing them to your product buy page— and that person buys your product or service—you assign a credit to the affiliate who sent them to you. This is the general idea behind affiliate marketing. If you get a million affiliates to sell your products, you will increase your website traffic and some of these visitors will end up buying your products. This type of marketing can be very productive. It is not simple to set up, so I would suggest that you get help and guidance from your business coach or webmaster.

7 BUSINESS PLANNING

Developing a formal business plan is a crucial step in starting your own business. This chapter provides you with a brief overview of the business planning process. Other than the financial section, this is probably the least "sexy" of the different sections in this book. It is certainly a topic that I see time and time again avoided like the plague. The good news is that this chapter contains a lot of great information, and you can find tools at the end of this book, and of course at our website, *www.moreprofitlesstime.net*. These tools will help make the learning process easier and faster than you thought possible.

Simply answer the questions in the Self-Assessment section and *voila!* You have the outlines for your first business plan and you are one step closer to creating the sort of strategic business plan your bank will want to see in detail (and ad nauseum).

I have been asked why I put this at the end of this book and quite frankly it's for one simple yet powerful reason: *Understanding*. If you don't understand and comprehend the information you have read up to this point, then how can you possibly—intelligently—plan and implement your business plan to give you the greatest opportunity for massive success?

I will present the bare minimum of plan components that can and do work together to form a business plan you can be proud of and one that gives you the flexibility to add to or adjust later on.

Are you ready for the home stretch?

Here we go…

Step 21: The Sales Plan

Many businesses (and I started one of them in the early days) enter the market without clearly defined objectives and strategies. Poor planning directly impacts your ability to sell products and services, particularly when there is strong competition from other businesses. So, it stands to reason that if you begin selling with a carefully developed plan, you'll significantly improve your chance of success. The following steps outline a very basic but powerful approach you should take to develop a sales plan:

» *Mission statement* – Develop a phrase or statement that describes an overall outcome for your selling activities, such as "to make my business more profitable."

» *Assess your situation* – Determine where your business fits into the market. You could use a SWOT analysis to assess your businesses situation.

» *Establish goals* – Build a set of goals that will allow you to capitalize on your opportunities and reduce the threats to your business.

» *Establish strategies* – Develop strategies and objectives to reach your goals that are

Specific, Measurable, Achievable, Realistic and
Time-measurable (SMART approach).

» *Delegate* – Assign responsibility for specific tasks to
your team.

» *Develop a plan document* – Organize the information
into a document you can distribute to your team and
use for guidance.

» *Achieve your goals* – Use the plan to achieve outcomes
for your business and reward your team for achieving
success.

» *Sales training* – Determine who needs to learn what in
both sales skills and product knowledge.

» *Sales tools* – Determine the tools and assistance that
needs to be developed or bought in to maximize the
best opportunity for success.

Your sales plan should be developed and adapted as your
circumstances change and your business grows. We go into
far more detail, and offer more tools at *www.moreprofitless-time.net*. We will also address these topics in future books.
Your sales plan needs to remain current so you can effectively
utilize it when making decisions and operating your small
business.

Step 22: The Operating Plan

The operating plan describes the *physical* necessities
of your business operations and includes information on
staffing, systems and processes, equipment, facilities, and
general risk management. Here are some of the components
of your operating plan along with the reasons each one is
necessary. These components blend together to give you a
solid foundation you can build a superstructure on.

People: Many things require consideration when
employing people to assist with the operation of your business.

As discussed previously, these relate to the hiring of staff, your legal obligations to employees, staff management and the termination of employment. The operating plan is a good place to formalize and record these processes and procedures.

Systems and processes: Planning and designing systems and processes for business operations involve the arrangement of management and staff, their roles and functions, and business administration requirements. It also takes into account business facilities and equipment, inventory management, and policies and procedures for other business functions.

Equipment: To ensure a smooth and effective business operations start-up, it is important to have the right equipment in place at the outset. This includes not only production equipment but also administration and communications equipment. The equipment you require for your business to become fully operational is dependent upon your particular situation. After determining the required equipment, you will also need to finance the cost of that equipment.

Facilities: Choosing the appropriate business premises requires careful planning and consideration. An inappropriate or poor location can be damaging to your operations, particularly where the business relies on ease of access or exposure to consumers. In order to make an informed decision when selecting a facility, you should keep in mind the needs of your employees, customers, and general operations.

Risk management strategies: Risk management involves identifying unfavorable events that could negatively affect your business, and developing strategies to overcome them. Potential risk events can range from minor to serious and likely to unlikely. This range includes:

» Natural disaster
» Departure of key business staff

» Key suppliers relocating or closing down, or a change in their credit policies
» Litigation
» Poor cash flow
» Family emergency
» A breakdown in occupational health and safety
» Bad debts

Here are five key strategies you can implement to cope with business risk:

1) Risk Prevention
2) Risk Reduction
3) Risk Avoidance
4) Risk Retention
5) Risk Transfer

To avoid making your eyeballs bleed and making you want to take me out for a beating, I won't go into too much detail here. I will just recommend that you get your business coach, accountant, insurance broker, and financial planner together to work out—as a team—those things you need to do better in this area. I meet with my clients' accountants, financial planners, business bankers and so on every 90 days so we can see where we have been, where we are, and where we need to be to stay on track with exceeding our 90-day goals. Use your team wisely, and if you don't have a team, GET ONE as soon as you can!

Step 23: The Management Plan

If your organization has at least one employee, it is big enough to require that key business roles be delegated to management staff. It is critically important to ensure you have a suitable management structure in place. You need to select qualified and experienced personnel inside and outside your business to fill the roles in your business. You should also be constantly looking for opportunities and methods to better manage your business and your team. An example of this is hiring a bookkeeper so you can focus on making more money for them to account for with your accountant and not trying to do tasks like this yourself. Believe me when I say they will do it faster and more accurately than you could ever possibly do.

To help you plan and develop a management structure and select the best people for each position, you should create a comprehensive list of the various tasks that need to be performed to run your business along with the responsibilities involved for each function. For example, such a task would be "Supervision of employees." You can then establish key management positions and assign roles and responsibilities to each position. This will help you match up suitable personnel to each management function and map out what I like to refer to as "who is who in the zoo."

Once you have defined the key management positions, their relevant requirements, and task descriptions, you can develop this into a formal "Job Description" document.

Job descriptions provide the opportunity to clearly communicate each individual's roles and responsibilities in the organization and overall scheme of the company. They also serve as a good baseline so you can more accurately measure performance. Do this by establishing Key Performance Indicators (KPIs).

A job description generally includes the following:
- » Duties and tasks to be performed
- » Responsibilities within the business
- » Working conditions
- » Material and equipment the employee is required to operate

» Working relationships, teamwork, and individual work
» Reporting relationships
» Relevant performance indicators and measurement details
» Other relevant job information as appropriate

Organizational Chart

With the necessary functions needed to run the business, and the roles of key individuals in the organization defined, you can develop and refine the structure by producing an organization chart which can be as simple or as complex as your heart desires. I usually recommend creating an organizational chart with the positions you want your business to have in 10 years and then create position descriptions, duties, responsibilities, budgets, and KPI's for each one.

You may be asking yourself: *Why go to all this trouble if you don't have any staff members yet?* The answer is simple. You create this organizational structure, and you put your name in every box in the organization chart until you start hiring people. Then see if what you expect for the position is what you can produce. As your business grows and flourishes, make sure it grows *how* and *where* you want it to and that the positions you define never become dependent upon one particular person, which can be dangerous in the extreme. If you are not careful about this, you face the predicament of becoming a total "control freak" and having the business overly dependent upon you or a select few key individuals.

The organizational chart is simply a tool that helps define the inter-relationships between all departments, divisions, teams, and people. It defines reporting structures and lines of authority and responsibility, and provides a picture of how the business functions.

Keep in mind that failing to define workplace roles and

lines of authority can create tension, miscommunication, and inefficiency within your business. People can be unsure about their responsibilities and who they are required to report to, creating inefficiencies and potential conflicts that will cost time and money.

Employee Motivation

Another important aspect of managing your staff effectively is *employee motivation*. In order to find, retain, and manage the people with the right skills for your business, you need to consider and identify those things that employees may be looking for in a job. There are a number of motivators you can use to keep your employees happily motivated, including:

- » Better work-life balance
- » Performance-based incentives
- » Remuneration packages
- » Training and education
- » Promotional opportunities
- » Different job designs (such as job rotation, job enlargement, job enrichment, etc.)

Step 24: The Financial Plan

Your business plan should include various financial elements. You will notice I am repeating some of the information I presented earlier in the book, but it is only because I want to emphasize the critical nature of this information. The financial planning section of your business plan involves explaining your situation with respect to the following elements:

- » Assets
- » Liabilities
- » Equity
- » Financial requirements
- » Securing finance

» Profit and loss statement
» Balance Ssheet
» Cash flow statement
» Budgets

All of these critical components should be included in the plan. I will discuss each topic in turn.

Assets: Assets are items owned by your business that have a commercial value and are used to generate revenue, such as cash, inventory, production machinery and office equipment.

Liabilities: Liabilities are financial obligations that your business has to its creditors, such as loans and purchases made on credit.

Equity: Equity is the amount left over after you have deducted total liabilities from total assets. It is classified into two categories; capital contributions and retained earnings. This number gives an approximate value of your business.

Financial Requirements: Your financial requirements include all the potential costs you will face in starting up a new business. These include the start-up costs, the ongoing costs, and the initial working capital for the early stages of your business.

Securing Finance: Securing suitable finance for your business involves identifying available sources of finance, understanding potential government grants and assistance, assessing the available financing options and understanding the typical requirements you need to prepare for when applying for finance.

Profit and Loss Statement: A profit and loss statement (also known as an income statement or a statement of financial performance), communicates the profitability of your business during a particular financial period.

Balance Sheet: The balance sheet (also known as the statement for financial position), provides you with the "net worth" of your business assets and liabilities at a certain date.

Cash Flow Statement: The statement of cash flows represents the cash inflows and outflows from business activities during the reporting period. Cash inflows are all the cash the business *receives* during the period, and cash outflows are all the cash the business *expends* during the period.

Budgets: Budgets are used as a planning tool to plan and predict future income inflows and expenditures. They are also used to benchmark performance as a point of comparison between expected and actual income and expenditure. Budgets should also be used when applying for financing using various projection periods and to represent what you plan to use the financing for in order to maximize your business success and generate a positive net income.

Step 25: The Action Plan

This is not a "think about it" plan or a "plan you write and stick on the shelf to collect dust" plan; rather, it is an Action Plan that integrates all of the strategies you have developed throughout the business planning process into a highly organized and prioritized plan of action designed to achieve your stated business mission and goals. This is achieved by breaking down the strategies you developed into small, achievable steps and then identifying the actions you need to take for each step. It can be used as a short-term (6 to 12 months) action plan to achieve short-term business goals, a medium-term action plan (2 to 3 years), or a long-term action plan (3 to 5 years).

An action plan identifies the business *goal* (what you would like to achieve) and the strategies that can be implemented to reach that goal. It also explains the specific actions required to achieve the business strategy. This includes the timeframe, roles and responsibilities, performance indicators, and alternative methods that can be implemented to reach the business objectives. The action plan should be reviewed at least every 90 days with your business coach and accountant to make sure you are on track to achieve your goals. Failure to regularly check on the progress of your performance against the goals outlined in the plan may lead to a result far different from what you had envisioned and quite frankly you may not like what you get.

Generally, action plans are limited to a small and manageable number of goals. This helps keep the plan realistic and achievable. For each action, you should identify:

> » The timeframe and priorities for each action.
> » The people responsible for undertaking each action.
> » Specific performance indicators to help you determine in the future whether your business has succeeded in achieving the business goal.

Once you have these details identified, you can formulate a series of strategies to achieve the goals of each action item. It often helps to break the various strategy tasks down into simple, specific steps to keep the plan on track and avoid getting overwhelmed or losing control. The first action you need to do is focus on the next few pages where I will ask you 20 very simple questions. In fact, they are so simple I have even given you a variety of answers to each question that you can add to if you want. Be honest; the only one you will be lying to, and letting down, is yourself!

SELF-ASSESSMENT CHECKLIST

8

Welcome to the self-assessment section, which will help you understand whether or not you have paid attention throughout this book. It will also give you a moment to reflect. In addition, this self-assessment quiz will help you evaluate your suitability to run your own business. At the end, have a close look at your answers and the responses you provided. The more honest you are in your answers, the more useful and relevant the information will be. When you are finished, you can use your responses to:

1) Judge if you are suitable for business

2) Identify your strengths and weaknesses

1. Why are you thinking of going into business?

People go into business for many reasons. Unfortunately, many start-ups are not successful and this can often be attributed to people going into business for the wrong reasons. Here are some typical answers:

» I need a job

» I don't like my current job

» I want to be my own boss
» I've always dreamt of working for myself
» I want a better lifestyle
» I want to be rich
» For family reasons
» I am not sure

2. Have you discussed starting a business with your family?

Many small business owners rely heavily on family support because of the time, money, and commitment demands. Working long hours with few, if any, holidays can strain family relationships. While not essential, family support may help you during difficult times and when you are heavily involved with the business. Here are some typical answers to this question:

» I have not discussed going into business with my family
» My family has no interest in the business
» My family could be described as lukewarm on the idea
» My family is very supportive

3. How would you describe your industry experience?

Relevant industry experience provides you with an understanding of the particular nuances of industry suppliers, customers, competition, key challenges, and potential pitfalls. Some say it is easier to get experience while working for someone else compared to "paying for your own mistakes" when you work for yourself. Talk to as many people as possible in the industry to realistically and objectively assess the viability of your proposed business. Here are some typical answers to this question:

» I have never worked in the industry
» I have recently started in the industry

» I have worked in a similar industry
» I have been working in the industry and consider myself an expert in this field
» It is all new to me, but I am keen to give it a go

4. What business management skills and experience do you have?

Business management skills and experiences provide a good background for operating a small business. If you lack skills in any areas of management, you may struggle to maintain the business at a high standard. It may be necessary for you to develop your business skills prior to starting your own business. Consider how you could either develop or gain access to the skills you lack through further coaching, training, contracting, or forming a partnership with someone who has the skills you require. Here are some typical answers to this question:

» People
» Finance
» Marketing
» Administration
» Customer service
» Production
» Distribution
» Planning
» Research
» Selling
» None of the above

5. What does your past coaching or training include?

Coaching and or taining provides many benefits to small business owners. It can give you the confidence, knowledge and ability to effectively plan and manage day-to-day business operations. Here are some typical answers to this question:

» I have had no formal coaching or training
» I have taken a few short courses
» I have undergone extensive managerial training and executive coaching

6. Why have you chosen this business and this industry?

Starting your own business involves a significant investment of time and resources. Therefore, it is important to ensure that the type of business you choose is a viable and profitable option in an appropriate industry. Here are some typical answers to this question:

» I have a great idea that will make me rich
» I have identified an opportunity in the market
» I can afford to start the business
» It looks easy to operate
» I am unsure

7. Have you prepared a business plan?

Preparing a business plan allows you to develop your understanding of your business by working through a number of important issues including marketing, finances, management, and legal requirements. Here are some typical answers to this question:

» Yes
» Yes, but it's incomplete
» No, but I am considering doing one
» No
» What is a business plan?

8. What do you see as the biggest obstacles in your business?

As a business owner, you will encounter any number of obstacles to work through and solve in order to be successful. The better your understanding of the potential problems, the more equipped you will be to deal with them as they arise. Here are some typical answers to this question:

- » Setting up the business
- » Developing a business plan
- » Lack of management skills
- » Finding customers
- » Selling
- » Finding suppliers
- » Operational issues
- » Finding help from a business coach, accountants, and other key advisors
- » Finance
- » Time
- » Personal issues
- » Employees
- » There are none
- » I cannot think of any at this stage

9. Can you accurately describe your targeted customers in terms of age, demographics, behaviors, and other parameters?

A business needs to have a good understanding of its customer base. A thorough understanding of the various types of customers you will target, along with their behaviors, will give you an advantage when it comes to utilizing your marketing strategies. Here are some typical answers to this question:

- » Yes, in great detail
- » Somewhat
- » No
- » Everyone is my customer
- » I don't know how to identify my customers

10. How will you promote your product or service?

Promotion involves making people aware of your product or service and then in some way encouraging them to buy it. There are many ways to promote your products using methods such as advertising, giveaways, packaging, event sponsorship, discounts and coupons, or on a website. Here are some typical answers to this question:

» I am unsure of what to do
» I am still considering the options
» I have defined a strategy to target potential customers
» I don't know anything about promotion

11. Why will customers buy from you rather than the competition?

For your business to become profitable, you will need to convince customers that you have something to offer that is better than what they can get elsewhere. There needs to be a sufficient reason for them to purchase from your business rather than from your competition. Here are some typical answers to this question:

» Price
» Service
» Quality
» Reputation
» Improved product
» Uniqueness
» Not sure

12. How would you describe the competition?

Understanding your competition will be important if you are to effectively compete with them in the marketplace. You should be able to describe their strengths and weaknesses and develop strategies to compete and capitalize on these points. Here are some typical answers to this question:

- » It is a very competitive market with many suppliers and a lot of pressure on prices
- » It is a competitive market with a few competitors but still some opportunities are available
- » There are few, if any, direct competitors
- » There are no competitors and my product/service is unique
- » I have not assessed the competition

13. How will the competition react once you start business?

Prior to going into business, you should form a projection of how your competitors will respond when you enter the market. Your competitors will likely implement strategies to protect their market share, therefore making it difficult for you to establish your business. Here are some typical answers to this question:

- » They will do nothing
- » They will observe and monitor my actions
- » They will advertise more aggressively
- » They will improve their service
- » They will start a price war
- » I am unsure how they will react

14. Do you have the right licenses and permits to operate your business?

To operate a business, you are required by law to have a number of licenses and permits. Your requirements will depend on what type of business you plan to operate, its size and location, and the industry you belong to. Here are some typical answers to this question:

- » Yes
- » No

» I am unsure of the requirements

15. Who have you consulted in preparation for your business?

There are many factors to consider before opening your own business. Nobody can be an expert on all of them, so you should think about seeking some external and independent advice during the planning stages. Some extra time and resources spent seeking advice could save you a lot of trouble later on. Here are some typical answers to this question:

» Accountant
» Business coach
» Solicitor
» Attorney
» Financial institution
» Insurance company
» Chamber of Commerce (America)
» Department of State and Regional Development
» Business Enterprise Center (Australia)
» Australian Securities and Investments Commission (Australia)
» Australian Tax Office (Australia)
» Office of Fair Trading
» Australian Chamber of Commerce and Industry (Australia)
» National Federation of Independent Business (America)
» Industry Association
» Intellectual Property Australia (Australia)
» None

16. Have you estimated your monthly expenses?

You should be aware of all of the possible expenses your business may incur during each month of operation. Before you can begin operations, you must ensure that you can meet these expenses while still making a profit in the long-term. Here are some typical answers to this question:

» Yes, I have developed a cash flow budget
» Yes
» Yes, but not completely
» No

17. Have you estimated your startup costs?

Startup costs can become substantial very quickly and are often greater than business owners anticipate. Having a thorough and realistic estimation of your startup costs, along with following a budget, will help you avoid this situation.

» Yes, I have a budget
» Yes, I am in the process of doing that
» No

18. Where are you getting your finance?

Depending on your business proposition, you may need very little or a substantial amount of finance to get yourself into a profit-earning position. Therefore, you need to consider how much finance you need, within what time frame, and where you will access it from. Here are some typical answers to this question:

» I am using my own money
» From credit cards
» A personal loan or house mortgage
» My friends and family
» I work part or full-time
» I haven't thought about it yet
» I don't know
» I can't get finance

19. Have you ever borrowed money before?

You may or may not need to borrow money to fund the startup phase of your business. Either way, you should consider your options now as you can't be certain that you won't be required to in the future. Your ability to borrow money provides extra security should you need to address any cash flow or unexpected expenses you may encounter in the future. Here are some typical answers to this question:

» Yes
» No
» I don't need to borrow money

20. What have you done to prepare for business?

Being well prepared for business will give you the best opportunity for success. While having a good business and product idea is vital to your success, you are unlikely to fare very well in a competitive market if you are unprepared. Here are some typical answers to this question:

» Talked to friends and family
» Attended training seminars
» Engaged a business coach and accountant
» Visited a business center
» Researched on the internet
» Talked to people in business
» I have previously worked for myself
» Nothing

ABOUT THE AUTHOR

John Millar is the Managing Director, Senior Business Coach Trainer and Consultant with More Profit Less Time Pty Ltd and CEO-ONDEMAND. Along with his many other business interests, John is proud to have been an associate of the most successful coaching team in the world.

He is recognized as a global leader and has been benchmarked against over 1,300 colleagues in 31 countries. John has over 25 years of hands-on ownership, management, coaching, and entrepreneurial experience in a broad range of industry sectors, including retail, wholesale, import, export, IT, trades and trade services, automotive, primary production, food services, transport, manufacturing, mining, professional services, the fitness industry, and more.

He has extensive experience developing and providing training for small to medium-sized companies and a variety of publicly listed corporate companies. John is an accomplished and talented public and professional speaker. He has been a mentor working with sales/management activities for businesses with a turnover under $100,000 per annum, over

$100 million turnover, and everything in between, with great success.

John currently works with business owners and their teams across Australia and has a "Whatever it takes" attitude that has enabled him to help his clients grow their business profits by up to 800%.

If you are ready to be coached by one of the best in the business, register at:

www.ceo-ondemand.com.au

Make sure to visit www.moreprofitlesstime.com and www.moreprofitlesstime.net for the new online Management Development Program: *The Business Essentials Series.*

DISCLAIMER

The material available in this book, video file, audio file or any other medium is distributed as a general reference source. While every effort is made to ensure that the information is accurate, users must be aware that some information may not be accurate or is no longer current. The author makes this material available on the understanding that users exercise their own skill and care with respect to its use. Before relying on the material in any important matter, users should carefully evaluate the accuracy, completeness and relevance of the information for their purposes and should obtain appropriate professional advice relevant to their particular circumstances. The material in this book, video file, audio file or any other medium may include views or recommendations of third parties which do not necessarily reflect the views of the author or indicate its commitment to a particular course of action.

External Sites

Any links to other websites are inserted for convenience and do not constitute endorsement of material at those sites or any associated organization, product or service. The listing of a person or company in any part of this website in no way implies any form of endorsement by the author of the products or services provided by that person or company. The author does not have control or responsibility for any external information sources. Links to other websites have been made in good faith in the expectation that the content is appropriately maintained by the author agency/organization and is timely and accurate. It is the responsibility of users/readers to make their own decisions about the accuracy, currency, reliability and correctness of the information at those sites. The author makes no warranties that external information provided from this site is free of infection by computer viruses or other contamination. The author accepts no liability for any interference with or damage to a user's computer, software or data occurring in connection with or relating to this website or its use or any site linked to this site.

Waiver and Release

By accessing information at or through this site each user waives and releases the author to the full extent permitted by law from any and all claims relating to the usage of the material made available through any medium. In no event shall the author be liable for any incident or consequential damages resulting from use of the material.

*ACCLAIM FOR **JOHN MILLAR'S***

Business Coaching and Training in their own words....

"Without John Millar as my Business Coach I wouldn't have a business today."

—Grant Jennings Managing Director, Jigsaw Projects

"Taking the decision to be coached and trained by John Millar was carefully considered after experiencing those who over promised and under delivered. I am pleased to say the content of his courses are the tools we all need to master as business owners. His delivery is engaging, thought provoking and empowering and after every session I came away re-energised. John always makes himself available for business building advice both via Skype and face to face beyond the scope of delivery. With his extensive personal experience in building small businesses, he knows and understands what it takes to establish and grow a business.I have no hesitation endorsing John Millar as an educator and business coach and the bonus is he is a very nice person."

—Anne Lederman Managing Director FB Salons

"Johns training with my management team was excellent, it was very different from the business coaching and support I have had in the past. John was clear, thoughtful and he addressed the issues we needed to cover without us even knowing they were being addressed! His follow up has been fantastic and exactly what I needed. I would recommend John and his team to anyone looking at getting some business coaching and training done"

—Wendy Crawford, Peopleworx

"In my dealings with John as our business coach, I have found him to be a motivated and insightful agent of positive change. He is able to burrow down to the root cause of issues and introduce effective forms of measurement. John then identifies and implements practical solutions and is there to provide the gentle persuasion required to ensure that results are achieved."

—Mark Felton, Lindale Insurances

"You have coached and trained us so well throughout the year that we are now used to & find it easy to prepare a 90 day plan, then break it down to actionable bite size pieces. Planning in business & personal life certainly is important. It allows us to identify the important things & the bigger picture. Thank you for your support & guidance throughout the year. And not to mention your insight, external perspective to review & assist our business moving forward."
—Linda Turner, Director Roy A McDonald Certified Practicing Accountants

"If you want to achieve sales results you never thought were possible and give your self a competitive edge my strong suggestion is to engage John services and listen closely to what John has to say, during the time I was trained by John I was one of eight sales consultants in a national business for 10 out of the 13 months I lead the sales tally and in 1 quarter I generated three times the revenue of the national sales force combined. Johns training and experience was well worth the investment and paid big dividends. Thanks John."
—Julian Fadini, Bellvue Capital

"John is a very enthusiastic trainer and business coach, he is very passionate about getting business owners and their team where they need to be. He goes the extra mile to keep ahead of the latest developments which he then uses to benefit his clients."
—Darren Reddy CPA

"I have been to a few seminars and heard John speak numerous times about sales, marketing and business. He is a very knowledgable and extremely enthusiastic business coach in all his interactions and I would recommend him to all business owners who need a sales and marketing boost!"
—Andrew Heath, Managing Director, Fresh Living Group

"I worked with John Millar and found his business knowledge, passion and innovation to be inspiring. He has always been able to set (and achieve) strategic long and short-term goals both for himself and his clients without losing that personal connection he builds with everyone he meets. He has been and I believe will continue to be a strong mentor and trainer for anyone wanting to take that next step in their business."
—Bree Webster, Online Marketing Guru

"Massive Action Day" – what an understatement, John Millars 4 hour frenzy challenged me to seriously review areas of my business I would not have gone to .... In this way, the process identified incongruence's in my mind, my business and my modus operandi. It's created a paradigm shift. Thanks John, the road map just got a whole lot clearer. Your friendship and insights since 2003 have been a gift to my business and I." —**Andrew Reay, Counsellor, Hypnotherapist and Counsellor, Thinkshift Transformations**

"John Millar is not your usual Business coach or trainer, he gets involved with you and your business and provides hands on help to make sure you follow through on his advice. He is highly motivated to help his clients and his personal guarantee certainly shows this. He has now transposed his thoughts, advice and love of good business onto a series of DVD's in his business venture – More Profit Less Time. This has excellent tips and advice for anyone either starting out or already in business. I highly recommend John to any business owner who wants to run a business and not a j.o.b.!"
—Darren Cassidy, Managing Director HR2U

"I and many of my Business Partners and colleagues have worked with John since 2010 as our business oath, trainer and motivator and found him to be an extremely motivational person to assist us achieve our business goals. This company and its products allows for John's skill set to be accessed by a wider number of potential clients. His very professional DVD series is extremely good value for money and is easily accessible for all of us who are time poor. If you are looking to maximise your and your business's results and to start achieving your goals and dreams, contact John; you won't look back!!"
—Mark Cleland, Mortgage Choice

"John develops real relationships with the people he comes into contact with. He is pasionate about what he does. His DVD and group training series, is full of good ideas and process to make you business better. Knowing what to do and actually doing it are two different things. John is excellent at helping you get things done."
—Carey Rudd, Sales Director, Online Knowledge

"I have known John since 2004 and found him to be extremely knowledable in both Sales and Business systems as a business coach without peer. John has provided me with business advice as well as personal coaching over the years, helping me with the running of my organisation. I'm impressed with John's DVD series where he has condensed a lot of the information in an easy to follow format that any business owner can use immediately. I wish he had released these DVDs earlier, as they are a goldmine of information, and practical how to that allow anyone to increase the profit in their business and get back valuable wasted time."

—Steve Psaradellis, Managing Director, TEBA

"John's DVD and workbook delivery of his no-nonsense advice provides a low cost option for those business owners looking to set and achieve goals that will increase profit. I found the conversational style of the DVD's easy to follow, whilst the requirement to pause the DVD and write down some action points ensured a level of commitment to the advice being provided."

—Mark Felton, Lindale Insurances

"I only met John briefly at a BNI meeting and knew instantly i need to hire him for my business as my business coach. His attitude towards work and how to improve my cashline had an instant affect on before, even before I finally hired him on an official basis. I found my self thinking "what would John do" and this was only after just meeting him. I can not see my business expend and give me "More Profit Less Time" without John's expert direction and training. If you want to succeed in business life, you need John Millar, without him you're just kidding yourself"

—Leslie Cachia, Managing Director, Letac Drafting

"John is the best thing that has happened to my business. I could tell you about the way he is on track to make 1/2 a million for me on his contacts alone, but that actually sells him short, he has become my partner in business, and cares about my success as if it was his own, we will flourish because I took the step to employ him to help me grow. If you get a chance to get him training you, dont wait like I did, get in as quickly as possible, his time is your business and if like me your business is to make money, then every day you dont have him on retainer you lose money."

—Russell Summers, Managing Director, The Give Life Centre

"I can highly recommend John Millar to any business owner who wants to grow his business. When I hear very positive feedback from colleagues who are skeptics by nature about John's ability and skills, I know John will help all those he comes in contact with. John comes with a selfless nature and the willingness to work inside a clients business to make it succeed. Rare indeed!"
—Darren Cassidy, Managing Director, HR2U

"I first met John Millar in mid 2010 and have always found him to be of an honest and generous character that engenders an easy association with him. I love how easy he is to listen to and how passionate he is about his work and topics. John demonstrates a love for life and his work and I have no hesitation in recommending his services." **—Kathie M Thomas, Managing Director, VA**

"I have listened to John speak on a number of occasions and find him a very knowledgable speaker with a passion for what he does. I have also interacted with a number of his clients and they all tell me that he helps them achieve results in their busienss. If you are looking for business help John is a person you can trust."
—Carey Rudd, Sales Director, Online Knowledge

"John knows his stuff, he knows how the get results, John has so many great ideas in building a business and helping business owners work less and make more money. John has released a DVD set on doing just that. I have watched the 1st one and it was great, very informative and easy to understand, I happily recommend John to anyone in need of help and guidance"
—Frank Eramo, Proprietor, Dynotune

"I have known John only for a short time, however the impact that he has had on me, not just my business has helped me to visualise opportunities that I began to doubt my ability to realise. He is encouraging and at the same time challenging so that he can/you can, begin to see how to maximise the business potential, John calls it being an unreasonable friend, I call it being a mate. If you have any questions about the direction of your business, if you want to seem your bottom line improve not just turnover but real profit, if you want a person who will work with you then I strongly recommend that you engage him at your earliest convenience. John is the best thing that has happened to my business. I could tell you about the way he is on track to make 1/2 a million for me on his contacts alone, but that actually sells him short, he has become like my partner in business, and cares about my success as if it was his own, we will flourish because I took the step to employ his training to help me grow. If you get a chance to get him training you, dont wait like I did, get in as quickly as possible, his time is your business and if like me your business is to make money, then every day you dont have him on retainer you lose money."

—Russell Summers, Managing Director, The Give Life Centre

"Its usually easy to be mediocre in business but it's impossible when you have John Millar training you. He has been my right hand since 2003!"   **—David Manser, CFO, Hydrosteer**

"I now have a commercial, profitable business and now its my choice when I work IN my business and when I work ON it and have had john helping me in business since 1988. I cant imagine not having John as a part of our business."

—David Wall, Director, D&K Transport

"The work John has done since 2008 coaching and training our marketing team, administration and finance teams, buyers, store managers and staff nationally has been fantastic."

—Ross Sudano, Director, Anaconda Adventure Stores

"John is a creative, professional, practical and committed business coach and trainer. His approach since we first met him in 1994 to working with a client team through the application of useful tools, information and anecdotes along with his easy going & easy to understand delivery sets him apart from other business coaches that I have used in the past."

—Anthony Beasley, Director, The Astra Group

"I have worked with John Millar for the since 2004 and I didn't think it was possible to achieve what we have achieved together. His business coaching, training and services just get better and better!" **—Terrance Chong, Managing Director, Echo Graphics and Printing**

"John's business coaching, training and support has transformed our business across Australia and New Zealand since 2008."

"We first met John in 2005, he is AMAZING at sales, marketing, operations, logistics, finance training and so much more. Since engaging John as our business coach our business has exploded, our team are happy, our clients are raving about us and my husband and I now take at least 12 weeks holidays a year, EVERY year."

"It's the no nonsense results driven business coaching and training focus John bought to the table that had such a massive effect on our business."

"We started working with John in early 2010, within 90 days of working with and being trained by John Millar we had the biggest and most profitable month in our 15 year history. That's impressive."

If you don't have John as your business trainer you aren't meeting your business potential.

"John has an extensive background in running successful businesses, plus coaching and training many business entrepreneurs. Combine this with his rare ability to communicate and present business concepts and ideas in a clear and simple manner and you have a winning formula. John has now condensed his knowledge and experience into this book. We all know how scary starting a new enterprise can be – there is much to know, and so much we don't know. In John's new book, the answers are all here, even to the questions we never would have thought of, until it was probably too late. I believe this book should be essential reading for anyone contemplating going into business."

"As an accountant I see so many business owners who simply focus on getting the work done, rather than operating a profitable and a sustainable business with the competitive edge they need in today's fast paced world. For this focus to shift, the business owner usually needs a whole change of mindset. I love John's down to earth and hands on approach when working with business. John doesn't follow a pre-defined and inflexible coaching plan, but rather constantly adapts his business model and resources to meet the needs of his clients. John will help change business owners mindsets and give them the tools and knowledge to operate a thriving business. I will be wholeheartedly recommending his book to my business clients". **—Coral Page, Principal, Knox Taxation & Business Services**

Many people have great ideas and eagerly think "I can make a business out of this: or think, "I want to get out of my job and go into business". Statistics continually show that 80% of all start-up businesses fail in the first 5 years.

There are so many components that make up a successful business, it's like building a jigsaw with an ever varying set of pieces.

There are however sets of rules that need to be followed and John has done an excellent job of compiling an extensive list of those constants and how to use them in this book.

John has an unwavering passion and commitment to helping small business success and in this book he calls on his 27 years in business himself as well as 15 years as a leading internationally recognized and awarded business coach to provide what I consider as one of the most comprehensive and detailed foundation for small business irrespective of the number of years in business.

As you read through this book take advantage of the additional FREE resources John provides, as these will be continually updated. So in fact you will have an ever-updating book.

Enjoy this book and the journey of turning your idea into a very successful Business. **—Steve Brossman, Voted the Worlds Number 1 Video Marketing Influencer for 2012, Amazon Best**

Selling Author of "Stand up, Stand Out or Stand Aside" and I am proud to personally add to the list - My Friend and Mentor.

That elusive pot of gold at the end of the rainbow, is the dream of all of us who take those first tremulous steps in starting out on their own.

What a gem of a "reference bible" John has assembled for the enthusiastic entrepreneur who seeks the thrill and satisfaction of being their own boss.

John leads us step by step through the highs and lows of business ownership; the thrill of success and the steady hand to guide the over confident.

This book is a powerhouse of information and advice for the beginner as well as a mine of information for the struggling hopeful who needs that extra "spark" to set them on their way.

I can do no more, but to congratulate John Millar in setting down a comprehensive and detailed step-by-step approach to building a successful business.

Good Luck; absorb the advice that John sets out; then hang on for the great adventure! **—Neil Harrison J.P., Multiple Business Owner, Entrepreneur and Investor**

p.s. Don't forget to take plenty of photos of the early days in setting up and getting established. You will look back on them with great pleasure and pride!

Congratulations on completing your book, "How To Turn Your Idea Into A Million Dollar Business."

I consider this book to be the "Business Start-Up Almanac" and essential reading for anybody contemplating the start-up of a new business. The book is in plain English and covers every conceivable task that a business owner must perform in order to survive.

There is attention to detail that most business advisers would either overlook or wrongfully assume that their clients have covered, even down to the importance of Trademarks.

This book ticks every box on my business planning checklist and I would strongly recommend to all small business owners that they read this book to at least confirm that they are not only running their business effectively, but have not missed anything that could cost them a fortune. And this is a must-read for any person contemplating the conversion of a great idea into a business.

The marketing chapters in the book will help any business owner to find hidden profits in their business. There are some very simple to apply money making strategies to suit any business.

The self assessment checklist in the final chapter is something every business owner should use to review their business on a regular basis to ensure that their business is in check and on track.

Well done John. I am sure this book will be responsible for saving many business lives. **—Peter Lawson, Best Selling Author and Marketing Architect, Founder of Biz Connections**

NOTES

NOTES

Lightning Source UK Ltd.
Milton Keynes UK
UKHW02f2057180218
318085UK00007B/131/P